DUE

The End of
Ancient Rome

Other Books in the Turning Points Series:

Turning | Points
IN WORLD HISTORY

The End of Ancient Rome

Don Nardo, *Book Editor*

David L. Bender, *Publisher*
Bruno Leone, *Executive Editor*
Bonnie Szumski, *Editorial Director*
Stuart Miller, *Managing Editor*

Greenhaven Press, Inc., San Diego, California

Every effort has been made to trace the owners of copyrighted material. The articles in this volume may have been edited for content, length, and/or reading level. The titles have been changed to enhance the editorial purpose.

Library of Congress Cataloging-in-Publication Data

The end of ancient Rome / Don Nardo, book editor.
    p.   cm. — (Turning points in world history)
    Includes bibliographical references and index.
    ISBN 0-7377-0371-7 (pbk. : acid-free paper) —
ISBN 0-7377-0372-5 (lib. : acid-free paper)
    1. Rome—History—Empire, 284–476. 2. Civilization, West-ern—Classical influences. I. Nardo, Don, 1947– . II. Turning points in world history (Greenhaven Press)

DG312 .R63 2001
937'.08—dc21   00-025740
                                                                      CIP

Cover photo: PhotoDisc
North Wind 14, 128, 136

©2001 by Greenhaven Press, Inc.
P.O. Box 289009, San Diego, CA 92198-9009

Printed in the U.S.A.

Contents

sors, the western realm itself underwent increasing divisions. Germanic tribes carved out their own niches in Roman lands and Roman leaders frequently fought among themselves.

fall of ancient Rome, a topic that still fascinates and absorbs scholars and ordinary readers alike.

Foreword

Certain past events stand out as pivotal, as having effects and outcomes that change the course of history. These events are often referred to as turning points. Historian Louis L. Snyder provides this useful definition:

> A turning point in history is an event, happening, or stage which thrusts the course of historical development into a different direction. By definition a turning point is a great event, but it is even more—a great event with the explosive impact of altering the trend of man's life on the planet.

History's turning points have taken many forms. Some were single, brief, and shattering events with immediate and obvious impact. The invasion of Britain by William the Conqueror in 1066, for example, swiftly transformed that land's political and social institutions and paved the way for the rise of the modern English nation. By contrast, other single events were deemed of minor significance when they occurred, only later recognized as turning points. The assassination of a little-known European nobleman, Archduke Franz Ferdinand, on June 28, 1914, in the Bosnian town of Sarajevo was such an event; only after it touched off a chain reaction of political-military crises that escalated into the global conflict known as World War I did the murder's true significance become evident.

Other crucial turning points occurred not in terms of a few hours, days, months, or even years, but instead as evolutionary developments spanning decades or even centuries. One of the most pivotal turning points in human history, for instance—the development of agriculture, which replaced nomadic hunter-gatherer societies with more permanent settlements—occurred over the course of many generations. Still other great turning points were neither events nor developments, but rather revolutionary new inventions and innovations that significantly altered social customs and ideas, military tactics, home life, the spread of knowledge, and the human condition in general. The developments of writing, gunpowder, the printing press, antibiotics, the electric light, atomic energy, television, and the computer, the last two of which have recently ushered in the world-altering information age, represent only some of these innovative turning points.

Each anthology in the Greenhaven Turning Points in World History series presents a group of essays chosen for their accessibility. The anthology's structure also enhances this accessibility. First, an introductory essay provides a general overview of the principal events and figures involved, placing the topic in its historical context. The essays that follow explore various aspects in more detail, some targeting political trends and consequences, others social, literary, cultural, and/or technological ramifications, and still others pivotal leaders and other influential figures. To aid the reader in choosing the material of immediate interest or need, each essay is introduced by a concise summary of the contributing writer's main themes and insights.

In addition, each volume contains extensive research tools, including a collection of excerpts from primary source documents pertaining to the historical events and figures under discussion. In the anthology on the French Revolution, for example, readers can examine the works of Rousseau, Voltaire, and other writers and thinkers whose championing of human rights helped fuel the French people's growing desire for liberty; the French *Declaration of the Rights of Man and Citizen*, presented to King Louis XVI by the French National Assembly on October 2, 1789; and eyewitness accounts of the attack on the royal palace and the horrors of the Reign of Terror. To guide students interested in pursuing further research on the subject, each volume features an extensive bibliography, which for easy access has been divided into separate sections by topic. Finally, a comprehensive index allows readers to scan and locate content efficiently. Each of the anthologies in the Greenhaven Turning Points in World History series provides students with a complete, detailed, and enlightening examination of a crucial historical watershed.

Introduction: The Rise and Fall of Ancient Rome

For many centuries, ancient Rome, master of the Italian peninsula, presided over an empire that incorporated all the lands ringing the Mediterranean Sea. The Romans rather arrogantly came to call that waterway *mare nostrum*, meaning "our sea." Indeed, "the entire Mediterranean Sea was a Roman lake," says historian Naphtali Lewis, "and those who lived on and around it looked to Rome as the arbiter [decider] of their fortunes."[1] The Roman state became so long-lived, entrenched, powerful, and influential that the vast majority of its inhabitants simply could not conceive that it might some day cease to exist. As late as the year 416, with the Roman Empire already in rapid decline, the Roman poet Rutilius Namatianus called Rome the "fairest queen of the world" and the "mother of men and . . . gods." The Empire's continued reign, he said, would have "no bounds, so long as earth shall stand firm and heaven uphold the stars!"[2]

Yet only a few decades after these words were written, the last Roman emperor lost his throne, marking the official end of the Roman state centered in Italy, the so-called "western Empire." In its place in the coming few centuries stretched a patchwork of primitive kingdoms established by the so-called "barbarian" tribes who had overrun the former Roman lands. Meanwhile, the eastern section of the Roman realm, centered at Constantinople on the Bosphorus Strait, survived for another thousand years as the Byzantine Empire; however, during most of these centuries its culture remained largely separate and distant from that of the West.

Modern historians generally view the dissolution of the western Empire in A.D. 476 as the beginning of the end of what we now call ancient times, or antiquity. In the coming centuries, some of the barbarian states grew into medieval kingdoms; and a few of these in turn evolved into some of the more familiar nations of modern Europe. (The medieval era is often referred to as the Middle Ages because it fell between antiquity and modern times.) The passing of Rome's ancient, long-lived, and grand civilization was therefore a major watershed in the pageant of Western history. As classical scholar Mortimer Chambers puts it, Rome's disintegration and demise "must rank as one of the greatest historical turning points in man's long story."[3]

Why Did Rome Fall?

Modern historians have churned out thousands of books and essays attempting to account for the cause or causes of this great historical turning point. The first major modern study, which remains the classic of the genre, was *The Decline and Fall of the Roman Empire*, published in six volumes between 1776 and 1788 by the great English historian Edward Gibbon. This large, well researched, and beautifully written work eventually delineated four major causes for Rome's decline and fall. These were its "immoderate greatness," or its having become too large and complex to govern itself efficiently and safely; too much indulgence (by upper-class Romans) in wealth and luxury at the expense of the state; the devastating barbarian invasions; and the rise of Christianity, whose ideas supposedly weakened Rome's traditional martial spirit. To these causes, later scholars added many more, including climatic changes that triggered a decline in agriculture; class wars between the poor and privileged; depopulation as the result of plagues and wars; race mixture with "inferior" peoples; the moral and economic ravages of slavery; and brain damage from lead poisoning.

Today, most historians favor two broad views of Rome's decline and fall. The first stresses military factors, the most crucial being the accumulative effects of one devastating barbarian incursion after another and the steady deterioration of the Roman army, which grew increasingly less capable of stopping the invaders. The second view (which does not argue with or refute the first) advocates that only Rome's political and administrative apparatus fell in the fifth century; whereas many aspects of Roman institutions, culture, and ideas survived, both in the Byzantine Empire in the east and in the barbarian kingdoms in the west. Through such continuity, this view holds, Roman language, ideas, laws, and so on survived to make the modern world what it is.

Whatever causes for Rome's passing one accepts, it is important to avoid a common misconception often portrayed in movies and other popular media, namely that the fall was a fairly sudden and calamitous event. Typical are visions of hordes of uncouth savages suddenly sweeping out of the north and looting and burning the cities and countryside. In reality, although some such pillaging did occur from time to time, the process was a very gradual one lasting several centuries.

Moreover, the Germanic and other northern European peoples who took over the Roman world were mostly civilized and some already partly Romanized tribes who for various reasons needed new lands to occupy. Most often their intentions were either to become part of the Roman state or to coexist with it, not to destroy it. Over time, however, the Roman areas they occupied became increasingly less Roman in character. More importantly, the central government steadily lost control of these regions, causing the Empire to shrink until there was practically nothing left.

Just as important as finding the causes for Rome's gradual decline, therefore, is discerning when that decline began. How far back in time were the seeds of the western Empire's ultimate demise planted? The following brief overview of Rome's history, emphasizing especially its last few centuries, shows clearly that the decline began many generations before 476, when the last Roman emperor was deposed.

Monarchy, Republic, and Empire

The early Romans evolved from a group of Latin-speaking tribes that descended from central Europe into Italy beginning about 2000 B.C. Well before 1000 B.C., a few of these tribes came to inhabit the area around the fertile plain of Latium, located in west-central Italy between the Mediterranean Sea and the rugged Apennine Mountains. Simple, agrarian folk, they established villages on seven low hills near the Tiber River; and in time, these villages coalesced (came together) into the city of Rome. Archaeological evidence suggests that this occurred within a century or so of 753 B.C., the traditional founding date calculated by later Roman scholars.

For an undetermined number of years, Rome, a small city-state only a few square miles in extent, was a monarchy ruled by kings. Their word was law, although they increasingly came to take the advice and respond to the demands of a small group of well-to-do landowners—the aristocratic patricians. Eventually unwilling to endure their subordinate role any longer, in about 509 B.C. the patricians threw out their king and established the Roman Republic. Roman citizens could now vote for their leaders, including the chief administrators, the consuls, who also commanded the army. However, the new government was largely controlled by a legislature, the Senate, whose wealthy, elite members (all patricians at first) set the policies the consuls acted on.

The Republic rapidly expanded in power and influence. Its increasingly highly skilled and disciplined armies conquered first its neighbors on the Italian peninsula, then the maritime empire of Carthage (centered in north Africa), and in time Spain, Gaul (what is now France), and the Greek states and kingdoms clustered in the eastern Mediterranean sphere. By the onset of first century B.C., however, ominous cracks had appeared in the Republic's structure. Powerful generals increasingly came to amass personal armies and challenge the government's authority. Among the most successful of these was the renowned Julius Caesar, who was assassinated by a group of senators in 44 B.C.

For over two generations, the Roman world suffered the ravages of a series of devastating civil wars, which killed hundreds of thousands of people and left the survivors fearful and war-weary. From this seemingly relentless strife, one man finally emerged victorious—Octavian, Caesar's adopted son. After he had defeated his last rivals, the Roman general Mark Antony and Egypt's Queen Cleopatra, in the naval battle of Actium (in western Greece) in 31 B.C., Octavian was the most powerful man in the world. Bowing before that power, the now humbled and fearful Senate conferred on him the name Augustus, "the exalted one." And immediately

Cornelius Sulla, one of a number of power-hungry generals who brought the government to its knees in the first century B.C., attacks his enemies in the Roman capitol.

he began building a new, more autocratic Roman state on the wreckage of the now defunct Republic. Though he never personally used the title of emperor, Augustus was in fact the first ruler of the political unit that became known as the Roman Empire.

From Offense to Defense

Augustus and most of his immediate successors were thoughtful, effective rulers who brought prosperity and relative peace to the Roman world. And the period of their combined reigns, lasting from about 30 B.C. to A.D. 180, became known as the *Pax Romana*, or "Roman Peace." The five emperors who ruled from 96 to 180—Nerva, Trajan, Hadrian, Antoninus Pius, and Marcus Aurelius—were particularly capable and enlightened (hence the nickname later accorded them—the "five good emperors"). They brought Roman civilization to its political, economic, and cultural zenith, prompting Edward Gibbon's later famous remark:

If a man were called upon to fix the period in the history of the world during which the condition of the human race was most happy and prosperous, he would without hesitation name that which elapsed from the accession of Nerva to the death of Aurelius. . . . Their united reigns are possibly the only period of history in which the happiness of a great people was the sole object of government.[4]

Under Trajan (reigned 98–117), the Empire was larger than it had ever been or ever would be. It stretched from the Atlantic Ocean in the west to the Persian Gulf in the east, and from north Africa in the south to central Britain in the north, a colossal realm encompassing some 3.5 million square miles and 100 million people.

Ironically, it was during these years, among the most successful in Rome's long history, that the seeds of its later destruction took firm root. Since the early Republic, Rome's overall military strategy had been largely offensive, stimulating a steady expansion of the realm. The usual scenario was for the Romans to defeat a people, consolidate their territory, and then Romanize and absorb them, thereby expanding Roman frontiers. Late in Augustus's reign, however, came the first signs of the fateful transition to a defensive military posture.

In the early years of Augustus's reign, the Empire's northern border was a ragged, ill-defined frontier that ran west-to-east through south-central Europe. Over the centuries, some of the Germanic tribes who inhabited the region north of that border had periodically pressed southward and threatened Roman territory. Like other Roman leaders, Augustus felt that the Germans' close proximity to the Roman heartland was dangerous and intolerable. So he set about pushing the northern borders back; beginning in the mid-20s B.C., his armies slowly advanced northward, establishing new towns in the areas they secured. These campaigns increased in size and speed. And after several years of intermittent fighting, Roman territory extended to the Danube River, prompting the creation of some new provinces.

The frontier then remained relatively quiet for a few years, until Augustus sent an official named Publius Quinctilius Varus to turn a section of Germany into still another new province. In A.D. 9, in the dense Teutoburg Forest (some eighty miles east of the Rhine River), a large force of Germans ambushed Varus and his 15,000 troops, killing them almost to the last man. According to the first-century A.D. Roman historian Suetonius, Augustus "took the disaster so deeply to heart that he left his hair and beard untrimmed for months; he would often beat his head on a door, shouting: 'Quinctilius Varus, give me back my legions!'"[5] Varus could not give the legions back, of course. And the fact was that no one, including Augustus, could replace them. Raising, outfitting, and training three entire legions was too expensive a proposition, even for someone as wealthy as the emperor.

More importantly, Varus's defeat ended up having important consequences for Rome's future. In the years immediately following it, the Romans became discouraged, wrote off Germany as a loss, and pulled their forces back, allowing the natives to maintain control of the area. The result was that Germany was not absorbed into the Empire and thoroughly Romanized. Permanently retaining their independence, the northern tribes would prove an increasingly dangerous threat in the centuries to come. (In view of their final triumph over Rome, the encounter in the Teutoburg Forest ranks as one of the most crucial and decisive battles in world history.)

The Century of Crisis

That Roman leaders recognized the threat the Germans posed and opted for a defensive strategy to keep them at bay is shown by the events of the second century. The emperors Trajan, Hadrian, and Antoninus Pius poured enormous resources into strengthening the defenses along the northern frontiers. They built numerous stone walls, forts, and guard towers, all aimed at keeping the so-called barbarians out. But this proved fruitless. Beginning about 166, several tribes violated the borders and Marcus Aurelius spent the better part of his reign (161–180) beating them back. Moreover, after his death many of these Germans settled in the northern Roman provinces, marking the beginning of the "Germanization," so to speak, of the society of that region. (This process, which scholars also refer to as "barbarization," affected the Roman military as well. Once these settlers had established themselves, many joined the Roman army, a trend welcomed by Roman leaders, who were always in need of tough new military recruits. The process, which accelerated in later years, eventually took its toll, particularly in a loss of discipline, traditionally one of the Roman army's greatest strengths.)

These developments during the otherwise relatively peaceful *Pax Romana* era proved to be only the first stage of Rome's long decline. In the decades following Aurelius's passing in 180, the Empire's political, military, and economic problems rapidly increased. And eventually, the realm entered what historians variously call the "century of crisis," "the anarchy," "the military monarchy," and "the age of the soldier-emperors." Whatever one chooses to call it, in the turbulent third century Rome experienced a severe crisis in which its political and economic stability was shattered. In fact, at times it appeared that the Empire might collapse from an inability to deal with a prolonged onslaught of serious external threats and internal problems.

The external threats included new and larger incursions of German tribes into the northern frontiers and provinces and full-scale war with the new and militarily formidable Sassanian Persian Empire, formerly the Parthian realm, on its eastern border.[6] Among Rome's internal problems during the fateful third century was poor leadership. In contrast to the honest and able rulers of the second century, most of those that followed were ambitious, brutal, and/or incompetent. Between 235 and 284, more than fifty rulers claimed the throne, only half of whom were legally recognized, and all but one died by assassination or other violent means. Another problem was a breakdown of military discipline, loyalty, and efficiency, as Roman armies frequently ran amok, choosing and disposing of emperors at will. While the generals fought one another, as well as foreign invaders, war and political instability disrupted trade, farming declined, and money steadily lost its value. As a result of these threats and problems, law and order often broke down, poverty grew more widespread, and life in the Empire became increasingly miserable, dangerous, and uncertain.

Emergence of the Later Empire

Disunity, chaos, and enemy incursions appeared to spell the end of the old Roman world. However, beginning in the year 268 a series of strong military leaders took control and, in the words of the prolific historian Michael Grant, "in one of the most striking reversals in world history, Rome's foes were hurled back."[7] In the span of about sixteen years, the emperors Claudius II, Aurelian, Probus, and Carus managed to push back both the Persians and the Germans and also to defeat illegal imperial claimants in various parts of the realm.

With the Empire reunited and minimal order restored, in 284 a remarkably intelligent and capable ruler named Diocletian ascended the throne. Modern scholars often refer to the new, grimmer, ultimately less stable realm that emerged under his rule and lasted until Rome's fall in 476 as the Later Empire. Like Augustus had some three centuries before, Diocletian took on the task of completely reorganizing the Roman state after a period of serious disorders. Among the first of his sweeping reforms was the transformation of the imperial government and court into an "eastern" style monarchy similar to those in Egypt and Persia, where the ruler was addressed as "Lord" and people bowed deeply when approaching him.

Diocletian also drastically overhauled the Roman economy. Because money was worth very little, his tax collectors often accepted goods such as livestock, jewelry, and food as payment. And to make sure that goods and services continued uninterrupted, he ordered that nearly all workers remain in their present professions for life. In addition, he attempted to regulate prices and wages, believing that such an effort would keep inflation down and the economy moving on an even keel. His economic edict, issued in 301, stated in part:

> We, who by the gracious favor of the gods have repressed the former tide of ravages of barbarian nations by destroying them, must guard by the due defenses of justice a peace

which was established for eternity. . . . We, therefore, hasten to apply the remedies long demanded by the [crippling economic] situation, satisfied that there can be no complaints. . . . We have decreed that there be established. . . a maximum [ceiling for prices and wages]. . . . It is our pleasure. . . that the prices listed in the subjoined [attached] summary be observed in the whole of our empire.[8]

Perhaps Diocletian's most important reform was the reorganization of the Empire itself. First, he divided it in half, he himself taking charge of the eastern sector and ruling from the city of Nicomedia (in northern Asia Minor, what is now Turkey). To rule the western sector, he selected a trusted general named Maximian. Then, in 293, Diocletian further divided imperial power. He and Maximian each retained the title of Augustus and appointed an assistant emperor with the title of Caesar, creating a four-man combination often referred to as the "Tetrarchy." In addition, Diocletian grouped the provinces into thirteen regions called dioceses, each administered by a *vicarius*, or vicar. The provincial governors reported to the vicars, who reported to three (later four) imperial ministers, the praetorian prefects, who, in their turn, reported to the emperors.

Although Diocletian's new system appeared neat and efficient on the surface, it masked two serious problems that would contribute to the realm's continuing decline. First, his need to divide the leadership among several individuals was in a very real way an admission that the Empire was too spread out, diverse in languages and customs, logistically complex, and poorly policed for one person to rule efficiently. Second, installing a new court and administrative center in Asia Minor laid the groundwork for a physical division of the Empire into eastern and western spheres. Over time, these spheres would grow apart, weakening the Empire as a whole.

Constantine's Revolution

Another important development in the Later Empire was the triumph of Christianity. As Gibbon originally pointed out, the faith's spectacular rise and the Empire's official adoption of it in the fourth century significantly altered the way many Romans viewed both military and public service. "There was undoubtedly a decline in public spirit in the Later Roman Empire," wrote the late, highly respected scholar A.H.M. Jones. In the early Empire, he continues,

> there had existed a strong sense of civic patriotism among the gentry [well-to-do], and they had given freely of their time and money not only to improve the amenities of their cities, but to perform many administrative tasks, such as collecting taxes and levying recruits [for the army]. . . . Under the Later Empire the old pagan [non-Christian] idea of public service waned and the church taught good Christians to regard the imperial service as dirty work, if not sinful. . . . Over a wider field, the teaching of the church that salvation was only to be found in the world to come and that the things of this world did not matter may have encouraged apathy and defeatism.[9]

Christianity owed much of its success to Constantine I, who ruled from 307 to 337. His predecessors, Diocletian and his co-emperor Galerius, were the last Roman rulers to stage a large-scale persecution of the Christians, who made up only about 10 percent of the Empire's population in the year 300. At this time a good many Romans still held the misconception that the Christians were dangerous fanatics who hated all humanity and wanted to destroy the established order. By contrast, for reasons still unclear, Constantine showed the Christians tolerance and accepted their help in his struggles for power. In 312, as he led his army toward Rome, then controlled by his rival, Maxentius, he supposedly had a dream in which he was instructed to have his soldiers paint a Christian emblem on their shields. This, the dream promised, would bring him victory. Sure enough, the next day, at Rome's Milvian Bridge, Constantine's troops, their shields bearing the symbol, annihilated Maxentius's forces. Thereafter, the victor became a strong supporter of Christianity (although he did not actually convert to the faith until he was on his death bed in 337). The Edict of

Milan, which he and the eastern Roman ruler, Licinius, issued in 313, guaranteed absolute toleration for the Christians and provided for the restoration of all the property they had lost in the persecutions.

Another of Constantine's achievements that was to have major and lasting effects on the Roman Empire was his establishment of a new Roman capital in the Empire's eastern sector, which was more populous and prosperous than the western sector. The inauguration of Constantinople, the "City of Constantine," on May 11, 330, was important for two reasons. First, it was a Christian, rather than pagan, city from the outset; and this did much to legitimize and strengthen Christianity, which became the Empire's official religion a few decades later. The state's eventual rejection of Rome's traditional gods and its embracing of the once despised Christian faith, all in so short a time span, constituted a veritable revolution.

Second, the establishment of the new eastern capital greatly hastened the permanent division of the Roman world into western and eastern spheres. The split became more or less official and unalterable in 395, when Theodosius, the last emperor to rule over both Roman spheres, died. His young sons, Arcadius and Honorius, now presided over a *partes imperii,* an empire consisting of independent parts. From this time on, there were two Roman governments, two royal courts, and increasingly two national policies.

The Empire Overwhelmed

Like the century of crisis and Diocletian's wide-ranging reordering of society, the triumph of Christianity and division of the Empire were major factors in the rapid ongoing transformation of the old Roman world. How that world might have developed had it had the time to evolve further will always be a matter of conjecture. This is because the pressure of tribal peoples on the northern borders, which had existed on a lesser scale for centuries, now grew to epic proportions; and Rome, with its economic and military apparatus unable to cope, was overwhelmed.

The human flood from the north began in earnest in 375.

In that year the Huns, a fierce nomadic people from central Asia, swept into eastern Europe, driving the Goths and other Germanic peoples into the Roman border provinces. "The Huns were indubitably [undeniably] frightening," writes historian Justine Randers-Pehrson,

> not only because of their Mongoloid features, their wild clothing, and their language that practically no one understood. Also frightening was their ability to dart around with lightning speed, which must have multiplied their actual numbers in the minds of their alarmed adversaries.[10]

The advance of the Huns set in motion the greatest folk migrations in history, as the Goths, Vandals, Burgundians, Franks, Angles, Alani, Saxons, and many other tribes spread across the continent in search of new lands. The fertile valleys of Roman Italy, Gaul, and Spain beckoned to them; and the Roman army, now not nearly as strong, disciplined, and mobile as it had been in the Empire's heyday, was increasingly unsuccessful in stopping the invaders. The province of Britain had to be abandoned in about 407 and in the succeeding decades various tribal peoples settled permanently in other western provinces. In 418, for instance, the Visigoths, led by their king, Theodoric I, invaded Gaul and set up an independent kingdom just north of the Spanish border. The western Roman government, suffering from increasingly poor leadership and dwindling resources, reluctantly accepted this loss and treated Theodoric as a "federate," an equal ally living within the Empire.

Only eight years before, Theodoric's predecessor, the Visigothic king Alaric, had besieged and taken Rome. This event had sent shock waves rippling through the Mediterranean world, for it was the first time that the city had been occupied by a foreign foe in nearly eight hundred years. The Christian writer Jerome (later a saint) cried out, "My voice is choked with sobs as I dictate these words. The city that has conquered the universe is now herself conquered. . . . She dies of hunger before dying by the sword."[11] This was an exaggeration, for Rome was still very much intact. The invaders plundered much gold and other valuables, but stayed only three days and destroyed few buildings. The situation was worse when Rome was sacked a second time in 455, this time by the Vandals. They had previously crossed from Spain into Africa, overrun Rome's fertile north-African provinces, which produced much of the western Empire's grain, and gained federate status in 435. Now, led by their bold and capable king, Gaiseric, they sailed north to Italy, moved up the Tiber, and ransacked Rome for fourteen days before departing.

The western Empire had by now shrunk to a pale ghost of the mighty state of the *Pax Romana* days. The last few western emperors ruled over a pitiful realm consisting only of the Italian peninsula and portions of a few nearby provinces; and even these lands were not safe or secure, for claims on Roman territory continued. In 476, a German-born general named Odoacer, who commanded the last officially Roman army in Italy, demanded that he and his soldiers be granted their own lands and federate status. When the government refused, on September 4 he marched into Ravenna, in northern Italy, then capital of the western Empire, and without striking a blow deposed the young emperor Romulus Augustulus. No emperor took the boy's place; and the western imperial government, which had been barely functioning for decades, now simply ceased to exist. Soon afterward, Odoacer's men proclaimed him king of Italy and he, and subsequently other German-born kings, took on the task of administering the region. The city of Rome still stood of course; and life for its average resident went on as before. But the vast Mediterranean dominion that city had once conquered with such boldness and vigor had slipped quietly into the realm of legend.

Notes

1. Naphtali Lewis, *Life in Egypt Under Roman Rule.* Oxford: Clarendon Press, 1983, p. 11.

2. Rutilius Namatianus, *Voyage Home to Gaul,* in J. Wight Duff and Arnold M. Duff, trans., *Minor Latin Poets.* Cambridge, MA: Harvard University Press, 1968, pp. 769, 775.

3. Mortimer Chambers, Introduction to Mortimer Chambers, ed., *The Fall of the Roman Empire: Can It Be Explained?* New York: Holt, Rinehart, and Winston, 1963, p. 1.

4. Edward Gibbon, *The Decline and Fall of the Roman Empire.* First published 1776–1788. 3 vols. Ed. David Womersley. New York: Penguin Books, 1994, vol. 1, pp. 101, 103.

5. Suetonius, *Lives of the Twelve Caesars,* published as *The Twelve Caesars.* Trans. Robert Graves, rev. Michael Grant. New York: Penguin Books, 1979, p. 65.

6. For some 400 years, much of the Near East lying beyond the Roman provinces in Asia Minor and Palestine had been under the control of the Parthian Empire. In A.D. 226, the last Parthian king, Artabanus V, was overthrown by Ardashir, who hailed from Fars, on the northern shore of the Persian Gulf, the region that had been the heartland of the old Persian Empire that the Greek conqueror Alexander the Great had destroyed in the 320s B.C. Proclaiming himself heir to old Persia, Ardashir established the Sassanian realm, which revived Persian religion and customs and adopted a policy of expelling foreigners, including the Romans, from much of the Near East.

7. Michael Grant, *The Fall of the Roman Empire.* New York: Macmillan, 1990, p. 3.

8. Diocletian, *Economic Edict,* quoted in Paul J. Alexander, ed., *The Ancient World: To 300 A.D.* New York: Macmillan, 1963, pp. 310–12.

9. A.H.M. Jones, *The Decline of the Ancient World.* London: Longman Group, 1966, p. 369.

10. Justine Davis Randers-Pehrson, *Barbarians and Romans: The Birth Struggle of Europe, A.D. 400–700.* Norman: University of Oklahoma Press, 1983, p. 42.

11. Jerome, *Letter 127,* quoted in John Julius Norwich, *Byzantium: The Early Centuries.* New York: Knopf, 1989, p. 119; also see F.A. Wright's translation for the Loeb classical library: *Select Letters of St. Jerome.* Cambridge, MA: Harvard University Press, 1963, p. 463.

Chapter 1

Rome's Near Demise and Temporary Restoration

Turning Points

IN WORLD HISTORY

The Empire on the Brink of Collapse

A.H.M. Jones

The dire crisis of the third century A.D., sometimes referred to as the "anarchy," brought the Roman Empire
nearly to its knees. And seen in retrospect, it constituted
the first major phase of the realm's ultimate decline and
fall. As explained here by the late distinguished Cambridge
University scholar, A.H.M. Jones, the crisis had many dimensions. Among these were poor leadership, grave military threats, a faltering economy, and a breakdown of law
and order. Professor Jones pays special attention to another important development contributing to decline,
namely the disintegration of Rome's old social order.

Many must have despaired of the future of the empire, ravaged by civil wars and barbarian invasions, exhausted by
ever-increasing requisitions, and depopulated by famines
and plagues. The root cause of the troubles which had for
two generations overwhelmed the empire lay in the indiscipline of the army and the political ambitions of its leaders. . . .
The second great civil war which followed the murder of
Commodus [reigned 180–192] in 192 had . . . serious consequences. Septimius Severus [reigned 193–211], the winner
in the conflict, knowing that his power depended on the
goodwill of the armies, raised their pay, increased their privileges, and by freely promoting soldiers to administrative
posts militarised the whole government. His last words to
his sons are said to have been, "Agree with each other, en-
rich the soldiers and never mind all the others," and [his son]
Caracalla [reigned 211–217], having murdered his brother,

obeyed the other two precepts. But the troops had by now realised that they were the masters, and in 217 a military pronunciamento [edict] overthrew Caracalla. In the next thirty-six years there were twelve emperors (not counting co-regents), not one of whom died in his bed, and after the accession of Valerian in 253, it becomes impossible to keep count. In every quarter of the empire the local armies proclaimed emperors: in Gaul there were five local emperors between 257 and 273, and between 260 and 273 Odenath, a citizen of Palmyra [a Near-Eastern city-state], and his widow Zenobia, ruled the eastern provinces from Asia Minor to Egypt. With the accession of Aurelian in 270 a recovery began, and the local pretenders were one by one suppressed. But he was assassinated in 275, his successor Tacitus lasted only six months, Probus, after a vigorous reign of six years, fell victim to another mutiny in 282, and Carus reigned only two years before he, too, was assassinated.

To add to the misfortunes of the empire, the pressure of the Germans on the Rhine and Danube frontiers was increasing during this period. We now hear for the first time of two confederations of tribes, the Franks on the Lower Rhine and the Alamans on the Upper Rhine and Danube, who were to play a large part in the ultimate collapse of Roman authority in the west, and of the Goths, who occupied the Lower Danube, whence they invaded the Balkan provinces and the Crimea, which they made their base for piratical raids on Asia Minor. During this period, too, a new peril arose on the eastern frontier, when in 226 the feeble Arsacid dynasty of Parthia was overthrown by Artaxerxes, who claimed descent from the ancient Achæmenid kings of Persia, revived the national religion, Zoroastrianism and laid claim to all the territories which [the Persian king] Darius had ruled more than seven hundred years before. Distracted as they were by their perpetual civil wars, it is surprising that the emperors were as successful as they were in dealing with external enemies. But despite all their efforts, hordes of Germans constantly broke through the frontiers and ranged over Gaul, Illyricum, Thrace, and sometimes even Italy, looting and burning; while on several occasions Persian armies swept over Syria, and in 260 a Roman emperor, Valerian, was taken prisoner by the Persians.

Money Becomes Almost Worthless

To the horrors of war was added financial chaos. The maintenance of a standing army had always proved a strain on the primitive economy of the Roman empire, and its budgets had been balanced with difficulty. Severus and Caracalla substantially increased the rates of pay and discharge gratuities, and the army was constantly growing as fresh units were raised by the emperors, either against their rivals or to meet the increasing pressure on the frontiers. Yet almost nothing was done to increase revenue: the only substantial increase in taxation was effected by Caracalla in 212, when by granting Roman citizenship to all free inhabitants of the empire, he made everyone liable to the inheritance tax which Augustus had imposed on Roman citizens. The assessment of the tribute, the direct tax on land and other property, was so complicated and rigid that it was left unaltered. Instead of raising further taxes the emperors preferred the easier path of depreciating the currency. The result was inflation [an increase in prices accompanied by a decline in purchasing power]. In an age when the currency was produced, not by the printing press, but by the hard labour of smiths, inflation could not achieve the speed of modern times, but over the years its cumulative effect was serious. Its extent can be gauged from the fact that the denarius, which had been in the latter part of the second century a decently engraved coin of more or less pure silver, had by the end of the third century become a roughly shaped lump of bronze, thinly washed in silver. In the early third century it was tariffed [valued] at 1,250 to the pound of gold; by 301 the official rate was 50,000.

The effect of the inflation on the population is difficult to estimate, but it was probably not catastrophic. The vast majority of the inhabitants of the empire were peasants: those who owned their plots would have profited from the rise in the price of agricultural produce, and the greater number who were tenants would not have suffered, since their rents, being normally fixed by five-year leases, would tend to lag behind prices. The shopkeepers and manual workers who formed the proletariat of the towns need not have been seriously affected, for the former would naturally raise their prices, and the latter were mostly independent craftsmen who fixed their own terms with their customers. The upper and middle classes, the millionaires who formed the senatorial order, the equestrian order from which the great mass of the higher officials were drawn, and the many thousands of decurions [local officials] who filled the town councils of the empire, all had the bulk of their wealth invested in land. Some part they farmed themselves, or rather through bailiffs, employing slave labour supplemented by casual hired workers or the services of their tenants; the bulk was let to small tenants, either for a money rent or on the métayage system for a quota of the crop. Besides land, the only regular form of investment was mortgages. Mortgages would have been swallowed by the inflation, but income from directly farmed land and from rents in kind would have risen with the rise in prices, and money rents could be put up every five years. As a whole, therefore, the propertied classes would have suffered little, though no doubt some families, which had invested excessively in mortgages, or could not adjust their rents sufficiently rapidly to their rising scales of expenditure, were ruined, and the profiteers of the age, men who had made fortunes in government service, snapped up their estates.

A Cash-Poor Government

The party most severely hit by the inflation was the government itself, and its salaried and wage-earning servants, more particularly the lower civil servants and the rank and file of the army, who had no other resource than their pay. Taxes brought in only the same nominal amount: the pay therefore of civil servants and soldiers could not be raised, and they found that it bought them less and less. Soldiers could, and did, help themselves by looting, and civil servants by corruption and extortion: it was during this period that the custom grew up whereby civil servants charged fees to the public for every act they performed—even the tax collector demanded a fee from the taxpayer for the favour of granting a receipt. On its side the government, though it did not raise the regular scale of pay, distributed special bonuses, or donatives, at more and more frequent intervals. Such donatives had long been customary on the accession of an emperor, and on special occasions such as triumphs. Now that emperors succeeded one another so rapidly, donatives naturally became more frequent. Should any emperor survive five years, it became customary to celebrate the event with a donative. The money for these distributions was procured by the "free-will offerings" of the senate, and the "crown money" voted by all the town councils of the empire; these, being arbitrary exactions, could be increased in nominal value as the currency fell, or collected in gold bullion. And in the second place the government made free issues of rations and of uniforms both to the troops and to the civil service, obtaining the necessary supplies by requisitioning them from the public. By the end of the third century, rations (*annona*) had become, apart from irregular donatives, the substantial part of a soldier's or civil servant's pay, so much so that officers and higher officials were granted double or multiple rations, the surplus from which, after maintaining their families and slaves, they could sell back to the public. Requisitions in kind [i.e., in the form of goods and services] . . . had similarly become the main part of the revenue and the heaviest burden on the taxpayer.

Brigands and Famine

The combined effect of frequent devastation and looting, both by Roman armies and by barbarian hordes, and of wholesale requisitioning of crops and cattle, both for meat and for transport, was disastrous to agriculture, the basic industry of the Roman empire. Peasants deserted their holdings, either drifting to the towns, where they could pick up a living in luxury trades ministering to the rich—for landlords still collected their rents—or becoming outlaws and brigands: large hordes of these ravaged Gaul in the latter years of the third century . . . and even proclaimed their own emperors. The government endeavored to supply the shortage of agriculture labour by distributing barbarian prisoners of war to landowners, but by the reign of Aurelian the problem of "abandoned lands," which was to harass the imperial government for centuries to come, was already affecting the revenue and the emperor ruled that town councils were collectively responsible for deficits in taxation arising from that cause within their territories.

Devastation, requisitions and the shrinkage in the cultivated area led inevitably to frequent famines, and epidemics ravaged the undernourished population. It is very difficult to estimate the effect of these losses, combined with war casualties, on the population, especially as we have no evidence whatsoever on the birth-rate. But it may well be that the population of the empire, which seems during the first and second centuries, and indeed in the first part of the third, to have been slowly expanding, received a setback and, temporarily at any rate, shrank during the latter part of the third century.

The Traditional Social Order

Concurrently with the wars and economic dislocation, and due partly to them, partly to more deep-seated causes, there occurred a general unsettlement of the traditional order of society. This order had, in the second century, been based on a series of hereditary but not rigidly closed classes, which by tradition and custom performed certain functions in the administration, defence and economic life of the empire. At the top of the senatorial order was legally an hereditary caste. . . . It was the function of senators to hold the ancient republican offices and to govern the provinces and command the armies. The equestrian order [made up mostly of well-to-do businessmen], which supplied officers to the army and officials to the civil service, was not legally hereditary, and access to it was, in fact, freely given to persons with the requisite property qualification, whether their fathers had held this rank or not; but the son of an equestrian official, unless he passed into the senate, normally succeeded to his father's rank.

Decurions, or town councillors, were again not legally an hereditary class, but, in fact, town councils were close corporations which co-opted the sons of members, and rarely admitted a commoner, even though he had acquired the necessary amount of property. The position of a town councillor was financially burdensome, since he was expected by law or custom to subscribe generously to the needs of the town, particularly when he held a municipal office. It was, in fact, largely through the munificence [generosity] of decurions that the magnificent games and festivals of the cities were celebrated and the grandiose public buildings were erected which still impress visitors to southern France, North Africa and Syria. The position also involved a heavy burden of work and responsibility, since the council not only managed municipal affairs, but carried out for the central government many functions, such as the collection of the tribute and of requisitions and the maintenance of the imperial postal service and the repair of imperial roads. Nevertheless, the old tradition of civic patriotism survived, and service on the town council was, if not coveted as a prize, loyally undertaken as an honourable duty.

In the lower orders of society the army relied upon voluntary enlistment. Many recruits were drawn from the peasantry of the frontier provinces, but a larger number were sons of veterans. In the lower grades of the civil service the officials were either soldiers, seconded for special duty, or slaves or freedmen of the emperor, who were normally succeeded by their sons, born in servitude. The peasants, though legally the majority of them were tenants on short leases, in practice cultivated the same plot from generation to generation.

The Traditional Order Begins to Crumble

This traditional order of things was profoundly shaken by the troubles of the third century. At one end of the scale peasants began deserting their holdings, either moving to another landlord who offered better terms, or abandoning agriculture altogether for the towns or for a career of banditry. The sons of veterans tended not to enter the army, but preferred to live as gentlemen of leisure on the proceeds of their fathers' discharge gratuities, which usually took the form of land or were invested in land. At the other end of the scale, a large number of senatorial families were killed off or reduced to poverty by the executions and confiscations which often followed a change of emperor, and their places were filled by new men. Senators began to evade the traditional magistracies, which were extremely expensive, and to be excluded from the government of the more important provinces, and in particular from the command of armies, by the policy of the emperors, who preferred to entrust such responsible posts to their own friends, who they hoped would not rebel. The equestrian order was thrown open to the lower ranks of the army, who could now aspire to become officers, governors of provinces and commanders of armies, and finally be acclaimed emperors. In the middle class, both because the burdens of office had increased and the old tradition of civic loyalty was dying, decurions strove to evade municipal office, and sons of decurions election to the council. The populace still got their games, but building ceased, and the huge monuments erected by past generations began to fall into disrepair. What was more serious, the whole administrative system was threatened with breakdown, since it was by the voluntary services of the landed gentry that the imperial taxes were collected. The government insisted that offices must be filled and the council kept up to strength, and ruled that a candidate duly nominated must accept office unless he could prove a claim to exemption.

On all sides the old traditions and the old loyalties were fading. At no time had the Roman empire inspired any active devotion in the great majority of its citizens. Men were proud to be Roman citizens and not barbarians, but were not moved by loyalty to Rome to sacrifice their lives or their money. The empire was too vast and impersonal and the emperor too distant to excite any emotion except respectful fear or sometimes gratitude. The loyalties on which the empire depended were local or professional. The soldier fought for the honour of his legion or his army or his general; the decurion worked and spent his money freely for the greater glory of his town. The generals and administrators of the senatorial and equestrian orders were moved rather by the traditions of their class than by devotion to the empire. Now the sense of *noblesse oblige* [benevolent acts by people of high birth] was fading among the aristocracy, the spirit of civic patriotism was fast vanishing in the middle class, the discipline of the troops was decaying, and there was nothing to take their place.

On 20th November, 284, there was yet another pronunciamento. The emperor Numerian [reigned 283–284], who had been leading back the legions from an expedition against Persia, was found dead in his litter, and the officers elected and the troops acclaimed the commander of the bodyguard, Valerius Diocles, or, as he was henceforth called, Diocletian. In the following spring he marched westwards, and defeated Numerian's brother, Carinus.

These events doubtless created little stir at the time: the Roman world was only too used to proclamations of emperors and civil wars. But they were to prove the beginning of better days. Diocletian was to reign for over twenty years, and then to abdicate of his own free will in favour of successors of his own choosing, and during these twenty years he was to carry out a thorough reorganisation of the empire, which in its main outlines was to last for three centuries.

Emergence of the Grimmer Later Empire

Chris Scarre

After the widespread devastation of the third-century crisis, the age of chaos that had brought the Roman Empire to the brink of collapse, Diocletian's administrative, economic, military, and social reforms in the late third and early fourth centuries gave the Empire what amounted to a new lease on life. However, the new Roman realm that emerged under his leadership—the Later Empire—was far from the prosperous, generally happy dominion of the first- and second-century *Pax Romana*. Diocletian and his co-rulers forced most people to remain in their professions for life. And a majority of the populace were forbidden from moving from their farms, so that they were thereafter in a very real sense tied to the soil. Moreover, the people were taxed heavily, mostly in kind (in the form of goods and services). This informative essay by Chris Scarre, Deputy Director of the McDonald Institute for Archaeological Research, details Diocletian's reign, including the Christian persecutions that that took place in these years. These persecutions, the most severe in Roman history, had the unexpected effect of strengthening the faith they were designed to wipe out; and by paving the way for Christianity's triumph, they ultimately hastened the decline of the old Roman world and rise of the medieval one.

Diocletian was an author of crimes and a deviser of evil; he ruined everything and could not even keep his hands from God. In his greed and anxiety he turned the world upside down. He appointed three men to share his rule, dividing the world into four parts and multiplying the armies, since each of the four strove to have a far

Excerpted from *Chronicle of the Roman Emperors*, by Chris Scarre. Copyright ©1995 by Chris Scarre. Reprinted with permission from Thames & Hudson.

larger number of troops than previous emperors had had when they were governing the state alone.

Lactantius *On the Deaths of the Persecutors* 7

With this mixture of falsehood and exaggeration does the Christian polemicist Lactantius describe the character and reign of the emperor Diocletian. Yet even Lactantius is forced to admit that Diocletian's accession on 20 November 284 marked the beginning of a new era in the history of the Roman empire. The successive crises of the previous 50 years had shown all too well the deficiencies of the imperial administration. Despite the prestige and achievements of [the strong emperors] Aurelian and Probus it was left to Diocletian to introduce effective measures to counter these defects. The most important change was the division of imperial authority among a small group of brother-emperors, first two, then the four to whom Lactantius refers. These were entrusted with the defence of different frontiers and helped prevent the rise of rebels and pretenders [to the throne]. The effectiveness of this policy is shown by the fact that Diocletian reigned for over 20 years and abdicated to pass his old age in retirement. In the eyes of Lactantius, any positive achievements were completely overshadowed by Diocletian's savage persecution of the Christians.

Diocletian was born on 22 December in around the year 245 in Dalmatia [what is now Bosnia], probably near Spalato (Split) where he later chose to spend his final years. He was of humble origin, perhaps the son of a scribe or maybe even a freedman (former slave) of a wealthy senator. Opting for an army career, he rose through the ranks to become part of the élite corps of Illyrian army officers which dominated the army and the empire during the middle decades of the third century. During the 270s Diocles (as he was then known) served as commander in Moesia, on the middle Danube. He accompanied [the emperor] Carus on the Persian expedition of 283 as commander of the 'protectores domestici' or household cavalry, a key section of the imperial bodyguard, and retained this position under [the short-reigned emperor] Numerian. We can only speculate what part he may have played in the murder of Numerian; if guilty, he successfully transferred the blame to Aper, the praetorian commander. Aper was an extremely ambitious man, but at the army assembly of November 284 outside Nicomedia, Diocles outmanoeuvred him and it was he who was proclaimed emperor by the troops.

The Elevation of Maximian

The defeat of Carinus [Numerian's brother and co-emperor] at the battle of the River Margus ten months later gave Diocletian undisputed control of the whole empire. Much to everyone's surprise, he sought reconciliation with Carinus's supporters, rather than revenge, and retained many of them in key positions in his own administration. Two months later, in November 285, he surprised everyone again by bestowing on one of his most trusted colleagues the title of Caesar, with control of the western provinces. The intention was to give Diocletian himself a free hand to deal with the problems of the Danube frontier, untroubled by the threat of invasions across the Rhine. Though he was a mature married man of 40 with a daughter probably now in her teens, Diocletian lacked a son on whom he could rely, and had perforce to seek the support of one of his generals. He chose well. Maximian, the new Caesar, was another Illyrian army officer, some five years his junior. The son of shopkeepers near Sirmium, he, like Diocletian, had risen through the ranks to serve with distinction in the Mesopotamian campaign of 283–4. He proved himself a loyal and able colleague to Diocletian, and what could easily have developed into bitter rivalry remained a relationship of mutual trust.

Maximian never forgot that Diocletian was the senior emperor, even when he was raised to the rank of Augustus on 1 April 286. Diocletian retained a veto on all major policy issues, and Maximian respected the wisdom and judgment of his fellow-emperor. They shared the consulship in 287, and imperial propaganda likened their respective roles to that of the gods, with Diocletian as Jove [Jupiter], the senior, paternal figure, and Maximian as Hercules, his agent in ridding the world of evils. Diocletian adopted the title Jovius, Max-

imian the title Herculius. They proclaimed themselves the
sons respectively of these two gods, and named their divine
birthday as 21 July 287. This divine parentage was designed
to inspire respect and to distance the rulers of the world
from ordinary mortals.

From Joint Rule to Tetrarchy

Diocletian spent five seasons 286–290 campaigning on the
Danube and on the eastern frontier. Already in 285 he had
fought against the Sarmatians; in 289 he did so again. The
year 287 was devoted to the eastern frontier and a show of
strength against the Persians. Maximian, meanwhile, was
engaged in similar operations in the west. In 286 he suppressed the Bagaudae, powerful robber-bands of displaced
peasants who were wreaking havoc in parts of Gaul. One of
their leaders, Amandus, even had the audacity to assume the
imperial title. Having dealt with the Bagaudae, Maximian
turned his attention to the Rhine frontier. In 288 the two
emperors mounted a combined operation against the Alemanni in which Maximian advanced across the Rhine and
Diocletian across the Upper Danube.

The story of these years was not altogether one of unbro-
ken success, for late in 286 serious trouble developed when
Carausius, commander of the Roman North Sea fleet, seized
control of Britain and pronounced himself emperor. Maximian attempted to unseat the British pretender in 289, but
his forces were turned back, probably with heavy losses, by
Carausius's powerful navy.

Despite the Carausian setback, the years 285–290 had
amply demonstrated the effectiveness of Diocletian's experiment of joint emperors. The only serious difficulty was the
question of the succession. In appointing Maximian as Caesar in 285 Diocletian had marked him out as his chosen successor. As time went by, however, Diocletian became anxious
to have some more formal arrangement for an orderly succession. Furthermore, he saw the wisdom of preserving the
device of joint emperors which he had established. The solution was for himself and Maximian each to appoint a junior
ruler or Caesar, who would succeed automatically when he

and Maximian died or retired. Accordingly on 1 March 293, Maximian adopted his praetorian commander Julius Constantius as son and Caesar, while on the same day Diocletian conferred the corresponding position on Galerius Maximianus at Nicomedia [in the East]. Constantius had already married Maximian's stepdaughter Theodora some four years previous; the dynastic arrangements were completed by the marriage of Galerius with Diocletian's daughter Valeria in June 293.

Victories in East and West (293–298)

There was trouble in North Africa, where a Berber confederation known as the Quinquegentiani ('five peoples') had broken through the imperial frontier. There was the still outstanding problem of the breakaway empire of Carausius. And in the east, there was a new threat from Persia, where the warlike Narses had overthrown the four-month reign of Bahram III in 293. In 296 the Persians seized control of Armenia from the Roman client-king Tiridates and began to advance towards the Syrian capital Antioch. Galerius advanced against him but suffered a heavy defeat on the plains of northern Mesopotamia between Carrhae and Callicinum. Poor judgment was largely responsible for this reverse, and Galerius was publicly humiliated by Diocletian for his rashness in attacking the Persians with an inferior force. . . .

Worsted by Narses in 297, Galerius did not make the same mistake a second time. Within months, with reinforcements from the Danube armies, he launched a surprise attack on the Persians in Armenia. The Roman victory was total; Narses fled the field but his wives, sisters and children were captured, together with many Persian noblemen. The treaty which followed was highly favourable to the Romans, who gained control over new territories along the Upper Tigris. The peace which it established lasted for 40 years.

While Diocletian and Galerius were fighting in the east, Constantius and Maximian were bringing the breakaway British empire to heel. The task fell mainly to Constantius. He began in the summer of 293 by recapturing the territories along the southern side of the Channel, including the major naval base at Gesoriacum (Boulogne). Carausius barely survived the setback; later in the same year he was murdered by Allectus, his treasurer, in a palace coup.

Constantius did not immediately carry the campaign to Britain itself, but spent three years making careful preparations, in particular by enlarging his fleet. The great invasion launched in 297 was a two-pronged affair. Constantius with one part of his fleet cruised off the coast of Kent, while his praetorian commander landed another force near Winchester and marched towards London. Allectus, caught off balance by these diversionary tactics, marched hurriedly west to meet the invasion but was defeated and killed near Farnham. After 10 years of separation Britain was restored to the Roman empire once more.

Victory in Britain and the east removed the greatest threats to the stability of the Roman empire, but did not end the almost constant need for military action on one front or another. Maximian crossed to North Africa to quell the troublesome Quinquegentiani. Galerius campaigned against Carpi and Sarmatians on the Danube. Constantius won victories over the Alemanni on the Rhine. But the major military crisis was over, and the key innovations of Diocletian's final years were all in the realm of internal or domestic affairs.

The New Empire

Diocletian's greatest legacy to the Roman empire was his comprehensive reorganization of the imperial administration. A two-tier system was developed, with provinces grouped together into twelve large 'dioceses' governed by 'vicars'. Provincial governors and vicars held no military responsibility. The army was given a separate command structure which cross-cut provincial boundaries, the aim being to make rebellion and insurrection well-nigh impossible. The new system worked well, and Diocletian won further praise for the introduction of impartial laws and regulations, for the safeguarding of tax-payers and for the promotion of a better class of men to run the empire.

The main losers under the new provincial structure were

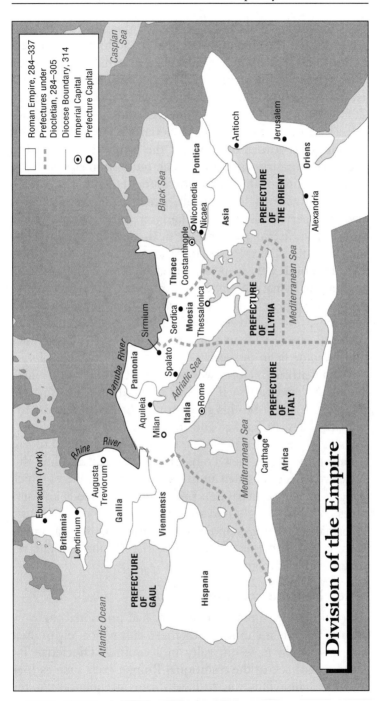

Division of the Empire

Roman Empire, 284–337
Prefectures under
Diocletian, 284–305
Diocese Boundary, 314
Imperial Capital
Prefecture Capital

the inhabitants of Italy. This (save for the immediate vicinity of Rome) lost the tax-free status it had hitherto enjoyed, and was divided up in a similar way to ordinary provinces. The senate, too, lost much of its power, and though Diocletian did rebuild the senate house when it burned down in 285, senators were steadily squeezed out of provincial administration. By the end of Diocletian's reign senators were permitted to govern only two of the provinces allocated to them by Augustus, and those much reduced in size.

The decline of the senate corresponded with a decline in the importance of Rome itself, which had ceased to be a major imperial residence by the later third century. It was simply too distant from the critical frontier regions. Diocletian visited the city only once for certain, in November-December of 303. Imperial government was in any case peripatetic by nature; the centre of power was wherever the emperor happened to be at the time. Nonetheless, under the tetrarchs, favoured residences did take on the trappings of imperial capitals: Milan and Trier in the west, Thessalonica and Nicomedia in the east.

Administrative reform was only a part of the battle which Diocletian had to win if he was to hand on a healthy and prosperous empire to his successors. There was also the urgent problem of finance and inflation. Diocletian comprehensively overhauled the tax system and endeavoured to halt inflation by issuing new coins of higher quality. When this measure failed, he issued an Edict of Maximum Prices which sought to fix the maximum prices at which goods and services could be bought and sold. It is a source of fascinating information on wages and prices at the time, but was unenforceable, and prices continued to rise throughout the remainder of the reign.

The Great Persecution

Most emperors of the third century had promoted the worship of the sun as a unifying theme, a cult which few of their subjects would have difficulty in accepting. Diocletian instead went back to the traditional Roman gods such as Jove and Hercules. This was to have dire consequences for the

Christians, who by now formed a large minority group within the army and the imperial administration. The first blow fell in 297 or 298, when Diocletian issued an order requiring all soldiers and administrators to sacrifice to the gods; those who refused were forced to quit the service. So matters stood for six years. Then on 24 February 303, an edict was issued ordering the destruction of churches and scriptures throughout the empire, and the punishment of leading Christians. Further edicts later that same year ordered the arrest and imprisonment of the entire Christian clergy; they were to be released only after they had sacrificed to the traditional gods. In April 304, a final edict commanded all Christians, clergy and laity alike, to offer sacrifice, on pain of death.

The anti-Christian measures were enforced to varying degrees in different parts of the empire. The western provinces, which were under the control of Maximian and Constantius, were scarcely affected. In the east, however, Diocletian and Galerius presided over persecution on a grand scale, as Christians who refused to recant were tortured and killed. Christian writers placed the blame squarely at the door of Galerius, who they described as, 'more evil than all the evil men who have ever lived.' They claimed that at Nicomedia during the winter of 302–3 Galerius argued long and hard for an anti-Christian campaign, and that after some hesitation Diocletian reluctantly agreed. It is difficult nevertheless to completely absolve Diocletian from responsibility for the Great Persecution with its lurid tales of beatings, burnings and Christians thrown to the lions.

The Final Years

By the time the last anti-Christian edict was issued, in April 304, Diocletian was already in poor health. He had been in Rome in November 303 for a grand triumphal celebration and other festivities marking the beginning of his 20th year of rule. In December he left for Ravenna, and it was during the journey that he became ill and had to be carried in a litter. He struggled on through the following summer, but in

December collapsed in his palace at Nicomedia. Contrary to expectation he did not die, but the illness persuaded him to take the extraordinary step of abdicating and retiring to spend his last years in the magnificent palace he had built for himself at Spalato (Split), on the Adriatic coast.

In order for the plan to work it was essential for Maximian, too, to abdicate. Rather remarkably, Diocletian managed to persuade him, and the two senior emperors gave up office simultaneously on I May 305, Diocletian at Nicomedia, Maximian at Milan. Constantius and Galerius became the new senior emperors, while Maximinus Daia and Severus were appointed to take their place as junior colleagues and Caesars. The tetrarchy was thus maintained, while Diocletian retired to Split and Maximian to southern Italy.

Events were to show that Maximian had not lost the taste for power, and was easily tempted to re-enter the fray the following year. For Diocletian, however, the retirement was final. He made only one further appearance in public life, attending the conference of the emperors at Carnuntum on the Danube in November 308. There Diocletian rejected the invitation to resume his position with the words 'If only you could see the cabbages we have planted at Salonae with our hands, you would never again judge that a tempting prospect.'

Diocletian died at Split, probably on 3 December 311. Lactantius claims that he starved himself to death. It is certainly clear that, despite the cabbages, Diocletian's final months were clouded by disappointment. During the summer of 311 his wife and daughter were expelled from the palace at Nicomedia and sent into exile by Maximinus Daia. Later in the year, many of his statues were destroyed by Constantine as part of a purge directed against Maximian. The retirement may have become a bitter pill, as Diocletian saw his prestige evaporate and his achievements called into question. But in the eyes of historians, it was this that set Diocletian most clearly apart from all other emperors who had held power at Rome: 'Diocletian . . . showed exceptional character inasmuch as he alone of all

emperors since the establishment of the Roman empire retired of his own accord from such an eminent position to
private life and ordinary citizenship. He experienced,
therefore, what no one else has since the creation of man,
namely that although he had died as a private citizen, he
was nevertheless enrolled among the gods.'

Constantine Ensures the Triumph of Christianity

John J. Norwich

The emperor Constantine I (reigned 307–337) was the prime mover behind two of the most momentous events in Roman history, indeed in all of history. Both ended up contributing to the gradual decline of the western Empire. First, his endorsement of and support for Christianity ensured that that faith would eventually triumph as Rome's official religion. The Christian views of a single, unerring god and a heavenly kingdom taking precedence over the earthly Roman Empire came to supplant Rome's traditional polytheistic faith; and the inevitable result was the steady disappearance of the old pagan world view. Second, Constantine founded a new Roman capital—Constantinople—on the Bosphorus Strait, the narrow waterway dividing the Black Sea from the tiny Sea of Marmara. Having both a western and eastern capital would eventually lead to a permanent division of the Empire. Also, the East was more populous and wealthy, as well as more strategically sound, than the West, which would contribute heavily to Rome's and Italy's decline in importance and the rise of the Byzantine Empire in the wake of their downfall. This well-informed synopsis of Constantine's achievements is by John J. Norwich, whose recent three-volume history of the Byzantine Empire received widespread critical acclaim.

Constantine I, Emperor of Rome. No ruler in all history has ever more fully merited his title of 'the Great'; for within the short space of some fifteen years he took two decisions, either

Excerpted from *A Short History of Byzantium*, by John Julius Norwich. Copyright ©1997 by John Julius Norwich. Reprinted by permission of Alfred A. Knopf, a division of Random House, Inc.

of which alone would have changed the future of the civilized world. The first was to adopt Christianity as the official religion of the Roman Empire. The second was to transfer the capital of that Empire from Rome to the new city which he was building on the site of old Byzantium and which was to be known, for the next sixteen centuries, by his name: Constantinople. Together, these two decisions and their consequences have given him a serious claim to be considered—excepting only Jesus Christ, the Buddha and the Prophet Mohammed—the most influential man in all history; and with him our story begins.

He was born around AD 274. His father Constantius—nicknamed 'Chlorus', the Pale—was already one of the most brilliant and successful generals in the Empire; his mother Helena was a humble innkeeper's daughter from Bithynia. . . . In 293 the Emperor Diocletian decided to split the imperial power into four, keeping the East for himself and entrusting the other three regions to an old comrade-in-arms, Maximian; to a rough, brutal professional soldier from Thrace named Galerius; and to Constantius Chlorus. Even at the time, the drawbacks of such an arrangement must have been obvious. However much Diocletian might emphasize that the Empire still remained single and undivided, sooner or later splits were inevitable. For some years all went smoothly enough—years which the young Constantine spent at Diocletian's court; but then, in 305, there occurred an event unparalleled in this history of the Roman Empire: the voluntary abdication of the Emperor. After twenty years on the imperial throne, Diocletian withdrew from the world, forcing an intensely unwilling Maximian to abdicate with him.

Galerius and Constantius Chlorus—who had by now abandoned Helena to marry Maximian's adopted stepdaughter Theodora—were proclaimed Augusti (the two senior Emperors), but the appointment of their successors, the two new Caesars, was disputed; and Constantine, finding himself passed over and fearing for his life, fled at night from Galerius's court at Nicomedia to join his father at Boulogne [in Gaul], where he was preparing a new expedition to Britain. Father and son crossed the Channel together; shortly afterwards, however, on 25 July 306, Constantius died at York; there and then the local legions clasped the imperial purple toga around Constantine's shoulders, raised him on their shields and cheered him to the echo.

Still needing official recognition, Constantine now sent to Galerius at Nicomedia, together with the official notification of his father's death, a portrait of himself with the attributes of Augustus of the West. Galerius, however, refused point-blank to recognize the young rebel—for such, in fact, Constantine unquestionably was—as an Augustus. He was prepared, reluctantly, to acknowledge him as Caesar; but that was all. For Constantine, it was enough—for the present. He remained in Gaul and Britain for the next six years, governing those provinces on the whole wisely and well. This rectitude did not, however, prevent him from putting aside his first wife in 307 in order to make an infinitely more distinguished alliance—with Fausta, the daughter of the old Emperor Maximian. The latter had by now revoked his involuntary abdication of two years before, had resumed the purple and made common cause with his son Maxentius; together the two had won over the whole of Italy to their cause. The marriage was therefore diplomatically advantageous to both sides: for Maximian and Maxentius it meant that they could probably count on Constantine's alliance, while the latter for his part could now claim family links with two Emperors instead of one.

Constantine Versus Maxentius

How long Constantine would have been content to rule this relatively remote corner of the Empire we cannot tell; for in April 311 Galerius, the senior Augustus, died. . . . His death left three men sharing the supreme power: Licinius, one of the late Emperor's old drinking companions, who was now ruling Illyria, Thrace and the Danube provinces; his nephew Maximin Daia, whom he had named Caesar in 305 and who now took over the eastern part of the Empire; and Constantine himself. But there was a fourth who, though not technically of imperial rank, had long felt himself to be unjustly deprived of his rightful throne: this was Galerius's son-in-law

Maxentius. As the son of the old Emperor Maximian, Maxentius had long hated his brilliant young brother-in-law. He was now as powerful as any of his three rivals—powerful enough, indeed, to take his father's death as a pretext for branding Constantine a murderer and a rebel. War, clearly, was unavoidable; but before marching against his adversary Constantine had to come to an agreement with Licinius. Fortunately for him, Licinius—already fully occupied with Maximin Daia in the East—was only too happy for him to undertake the reconquest of Italy on his behalf. The agreement was sealed by another betrothal—this time of Licinius himself to Constantine's half-sister Constantia.

Throughout Constantine's long advance, Maxentius had remained in Rome. Only when his brother-in-law's army was approaching the city did he march out to meet it. The two armies met on 28 October 312 at Saxa Rubra, the 'red rocks' on the Via Flaminia, some seven or eight miles northeast of Rome. It was here, as later legend has it, just before or perhaps even during the battle, that Constantine experienced his famous vision. As [the fourth-century Christian historian] Eusebius describes it:

> . . . a most marvellous sign appeared to him from heaven . . . He said that at about midday, when the sun was beginning to decline, he saw with his own eyes the trophy of a cross of light in the heavens, above the sun, and bearing the inscription Conquer by This (*Hoc Vince*). He himself was struck with amazement, and his whole army also.

Inspired by so unmistakable an indication of divine favour, Constantine routed the army of Maxentius, driving it southward to where the Tiber is crossed by the old Milvian Bridge. Next to this bridge Maxentius had constructed another on pontoons, by which he could if necessary make an orderly retreat and which could then be broken in the middle to prevent pursuit. Over this his shattered army stampeded, the soldiers now fleeing for their lives. They might have escaped, had not the engineers lost their heads and drawn the bolts too early. The whole structure collapsed, throwing hundreds of men into the fast-flowing water.

Those who had not yet crossed made blindly for the old stone bridge, now their only chance of safety; but, as Maxentius had known, it was too narrow. Many were crushed to death, others fell and were trampled underfoot, still others were flung down by their own comrades into the river below. Among the last was the usurper himself, whose body was later found washed up on the bank.

The battle of the Milvian Bridge made Constantine absolute master of all Europe. It also marked, if not his actual conversion to Christianity, at least the moment when he set himself up as a protector and patron of his Christian subjects. . . .

The Miraculous Vision

To what extent did the vision of the Cross that the Emperor is said to have experienced near the Milvian Bridge constitute not only one of the decisive turning-points of his life but also a watershed of world history? Before we can answer that question, we must ask ourselves another: what actually happened? According to the Christian scholar and rhetorician Lactantius, tutor to Constantine's son Crispus,

> Constantine was directed in a dream to cause *the heavenly sign* to be delineated on the shields of his soldiers, and so to proceed to battle. He did as he had been commanded, and he marked on their shields the letter X, with a perpendicular line drawn through it and turned round the top, thus ☧, being the cypher of Christ.

He says no more. We have no mention of a vision, only of a dream. There is not even any suggestion that the Saviour or the Cross ever appeared to the Emperor at all. As for 'the heavenly sign', it was simply a monogram of *chi* (X) and *rho* (P), the first two Greek letters in the name of Christ, that had long been a familiar symbol in Christian inscriptions. And perhaps more significant still is the fact that our other valuable source, Eusebius, makes no reference to either a dream or a vision in the account of the battle which he gives in his *Ecclesiastical History* of about 325. It is only in his *Life of Constantine*, written many years later, that he produces the passage quoted above.

What conclusions are we to draw from all this? Firstly, surely, that there was no vision. Had there been one, it is unthinkable that there should be no single reference to it until the *Life of Constantine*. The Emperor himself never seems to have spoken of it—except to Eusebius—even on those occasions when he might have been expected to do so. Then there is Eusebius's specific statement that 'the whole army . . . witnessed the miracle'. If that were true, 98,000 men kept the secret remarkably well.

There can be little doubt, on the other hand, that at a certain moment before the battle the Emperor underwent some profound spiritual experience. There are indications that he was already in a state of grave religious uncertainty, and was increasingly tending towards monotheism: after 310 his coins depict one god only—*Sol Invictus*, the Unconquered Sun—of whom Constantine also claimed to have had a vision some years before. Yet this faith too seems to have left him unsatisfied. No man, in short, was readier for conversion during that late summer of 312; and it is hardly surprising that, up to a point at least, his prayers were answered. If we accept this hypothesis Eusebius's story becomes a good deal easier to understand. Constantine had always cherished a strongly developed sense of divine mission. What could be more natural than that, looking back on his life, he should have allowed his memory to add a gentle gloss here and there? In his day the existence of miracles and heavenly portents was universally accepted; if he could have had a vision and if, in the circumstances, he should have had a vision, then a vision he had had.

The Sole Emperor

Early in January 313, Constantine left Rome for Milan, where he had arranged to meet Licinius. Their talks passed off amicably enough. Licinius seems to have agreed that Constantine should keep the territories that he had conquered, and was duly married to Constantia. Where the Christians were concerned, the new brothers-in-law settled the final text of a further edict, granting Christianity full legal recognition throughout the Empire:

> I, Constantine Augustus, and I, Licinius Augustus, resolved to secure respect and reverence for the Deity, grant to Christians and to all others the right freely to follow whatever form of worship they please, that whatsoever Divinity dwells in heaven may be favourable to us and to all those under our authority.

At the time of the Edict of Milan, the two Emperors were friends; but they did not remain so for long. For some time already Constantine had been determined to put an end to Diocletian's disastrous division of the Empire and to rule it alone. Open warfare broke out in 314, and again nine years later, when the two armies fought a furious battle outside Adrianople in Thrace. On both occasions Constantine emerged the victor; towards the end of 323 Licinius was captured and summarily put to death.

During the civil war Constantine had turned more and more exclusively towards the God of the Christians. For some years he had been legislating in their favour. The clergy were exempted from municipal obligations, while episcopal courts were given the right to act as courts of appeal for civil cases. Other laws, too, suggest a degree of Christian inspiration, such as that of 319 prohibiting the murder of slaves and—most celebrated of all—the law of 321 proclaiming Sunday, 'the venerable day of the Sun', as a day of rest. But in none of this legislation is the name of Christ himself mentioned or the Christian faith in any way professed. Now at last, with the Empire safely reunited under his authority, Constantine could afford to come into the open. There must be no coercion: pagans must be allowed to continue in the old faith if they chose to do so. . . .

He proved . . . assiduous in his determination to make Rome a Christian city. He endowed a . . . great basilica, now known as S. Paolo fuori le Mura—dedicated . . . to St Paul, at the site of the saint's tomb on the road to Ostia; and another—now S. Sebastiano—in honour of the Holy Apostles on the Appian Way. His most important creation of all, however, was the basilica that he commanded to be built above the traditional resting-place of St Peter on the Vatican Hill.

Constantine's frenetic building activity in Rome proves beyond all doubt that he saw the city as the chief shrine of the Christian faith, excepting only Jerusalem itself; and he was determined to do all he could to ensure that it would be architecturally worthy of its dignity. Personally, on the other hand, he never liked it, or stayed in it a moment longer than he could help. His heart was in the East. He had business in Byzantium.

The New Rome

When Constantine first set eyes on Byzantium, the city was already nearly a thousand years old: a small settlement was already flourishing on the site by about 600 BC, with its acropolis on the high ground where the Church of St Sophia and the Palace of Topkapi stand today. Inevitably, when his new city of Constantinople became the centre of the late Roman world, stories were to grow up about the supernatural circumstances attending its foundation: how he personally traced out the line of the walls with his spear—replying, when his companions showed astonishment at its length, with the words: 'I shall continue until he who walks ahead of me bids me stop.' In fact, however, at that time the Emperor was merely planning a commemorative city bearing his name and serving as a perpetual reminder of his greatness and glory. What decided him to make it the capital of his Empire was, almost certainly, his second visit to Rome, whose republican and pagan traditions could clearly have no place in his new Christian Empire. Intellectually and culturally, it was growing more and more out of touch with the new and progressive thinking of the Hellenistic world. The Roman academies and libraries were no longer any match for those of Alexandria, Antioch or Pergamum. In the economic field, too, a similar trend was apparent. In Rome and throughout much of the Italian peninsula, malaria was on the increase and populations were dwindling; the incomparably greater economic resources of what was known as the *pars orientalis* [eastern region] constituted an attraction which no government could afford to ignore.

Strategically, the disadvantages of the old capital were

more serious still. The principal dangers to imperial security were now concentrated along the Empire's eastern borders: the Sarmatians around the lower Danube, the Ostrogoths to the north of the Black Sea and—most menacing of all—the Persians, whose great Sassanian Empire by now extended from the former Roman provinces of Armenia and Mesopotamia as far as the Hindu Kush. The centre of the Empire—indeed, of the whole civilized world—had shifted irrevocably to the East. Italy had become a backwater.

The focal point of Constantine's new city was the *Milion*, or First Milestone. It consisted of four triumphal arches forming a square and supporting a cupola, above which was set the most venerable Christian relic of all—the True Cross itself, sent back by the Empress Helena from Jerusalem a year or two before. From it all the distances in the Empire were measured; it was, in effect, the centre of the world. A little to the east of it, on a site occupied in former times by a shrine of Aphrodite, rose the first great Christian church of the new capital, dedicated not to any saint or martyr but to the Holy Peace of God, St Eirene. A few years later this church was to be joined—and somewhat overshadowed—by a larger and still more splendid neighbour, St Sophia, the Church of the Holy Wisdom; but for the time being it had no rival. A quarter of a mile or so away from it towards the Marmara stood Constantine's huge Hippodrome [track for chariot races]. . . . Half-way along its eastern side, the imperial box gave direct access by a spiral staircase to that vast complex of reception halls, government offices, domestic apartments, baths, barracks and parade grounds that was the palace. . . .

Around the palace, the church and the Hippodrome, tens of thousands of labourers and artisans worked day and night; and, thanks to the wholesale plunder by which the towns of Europe and Asia were deprived of their finest statues, trophies and works of art, it was already a fine and noble city— though not yet a very large one—that was dedicated, as Constantine had determined that it should be, in a special ceremony that marked the climax of his silver jubilee. The Emperor attended High Mass in St Eirene, while the pagan population prayed for his prosperity and that of the city in such temples as he had authorized for their use. It is with this Mass, at which the city was formally dedicated to the Holy Virgin, that the history of Constantinople really begins—and, with it, that of the Byzantine Empire. The date was 11 May 330. It was, we are credibly informed, a Monday.

Only half a dozen years before, Byzantium had been just another small Greek town; now, reborn and renamed, it was the 'New Rome'—its official appellation proudly carved on a stone pillar in the recently completed law courts. In the old Rome, to be sure, the people kept all their ancient privileges. Trade, too, went on as before; the port of Ostia remained busy. But several of the old Roman senatorial families were already beginning to trickle away to the Bosphorus, lured by the promise of magnificent palaces in the city and extensive estates in Thrace, Bithynia and Pontus; and a larger and infinitely more sumptuous Senate House had risen in the new capital to accommodate them. Meanwhile all the cities of the Empire were ransacked for works of art with which the growing city was to be adorned—preference being normally given to temple statues of the ancient gods, since by removing them from their traditional shrines and setting them up in public, unconsecrated places for aesthetic rather than religious purposes, Constantine could strike a telling blow at the old pagan faith.

Problems and Struggles of Constantine's Successors

Michael Grant

In the half century following Constantine's death in 337, the Empire and its inhabitants experienced a number of struggles that increased in size and intensity. Among these was a bitter rivalry between pagan and Christian leaders. The most famous confrontation came after the state, at the urgings of Christian leaders, removed the statue of the goddess Victory from the Senate House; and the influential, well-spoken aristocrat Quintus Aurelius Symmachus attempted, unsuccessfully, to have it reinstated. As explained here by popular Edinburgh University scholar Michael Grant, it was during this same period that the barbarian incursions greatly increased in size and scope. The troubles attending these mass population movements led to the horrendous slaughter of some 40,000 Romans at Adrianople in 378. There was also the growing rivalry between the western and eastern Roman spheres, centered in Rome on the one hand and Constantinople on the other. No one realized at the time, of course, that these rivalries and struggles foreshadowed the end of the Roman world they knew.

Constantine's later years, before his death in 337, were marred by suspicions and executions within his own family, and he made the classic mistake of bequeathing the empire jointly to no less than five members of his house. By 350, after various wars, his son Constantius II (337–361) was their sole survivor. He devoted much of his long reign to attempting to transform Constantine's Christian revolution into a permanent reality. He himself, however, belonged to the Arian sect which held Jesus to be inferior in status to his Father, but was destined to be overtaken by orthodox Catholicism; and his attempts to grapple with the theological disputes that were splitting the Church did not prove effective.

His cousin and successor Julian 'the Apostate' (361–3) undertook a reversion to paganism, which proved too archaistic [behind the times] to prevail, however. He also sought to deal with the Persians, but this attempt, too, was never brought to a satisfactory conclusion. The Danubian officer who succeeded him on the throne, Jovian (364–4), reversed both these policies, negotiating an unpopular peace with the Persians, and restoring Christianity as the religion of the state.

The Last Effective Ruler

The army next acclaimed Valentinian I (364–375), another Danubian, as emperor: and he was the last truly effective ruler to occupy the throne before the western empire fell. Although cruel and choleric by nature, Valentinian was an excellent commander and organizer. He felt no affection for the Roman nobility, but was unusually sympathetic to the plight of the poor. More unusually still, he was prepared to tolerate differences of religious opinion.

Like Diocletian before him, however, Valentinian I felt that more than one ruler was needed, and in consequence he handed over the eastern provinces to his brother Valens, who took up residence at Constantinople. Valentinian himself stayed in the west, retaining Mediolanum (Milan) as his own capital (while permitting the Senate to remain at Rome).

During his reign, he found himself confronted by a succession of external crises, which he handled with efficiency. First, Germans had broken across the River Rhenus (Rhine), capturing Moguntiacum (Mainz). But Valentinian defeated them on three different occasions, and then marched deep into the interior of their country. Staying in the north for seven years, he reconstructed the imperial defences, successfully set various German tribal groups at odds with one another, and agreed to admit many other Germans within the western provinces. Next, in 374–5, he repulsed further

Ammianus Describes Constantius

In his history of Rome, the distinguished fourth-century Roman historian Ammianus Marcellinus includes some of what he sees as the good and bad traits of the emperor Constantius II, Constantine's son and principal immediate successor.

I propose to draw a clear distinction between Constantius' good and bad qualities, and it will be convenient to deal first with the former. He always maintained the dignity of his position as emperor and thought it beneath him to court popularity. He was exceedingly sparing in the conferment of higher honours; with a few exceptions he allowed no changes which would increase the prestige of his administrators, and he never let the military set themselves up too high. Under him, no general was advanced to the highest rank of nobility; as far as my memory serves, generals were only of the second grade. . . . In handling his army Constantius was exceptionally careful and sometimes over-critical in his scrutiny of men's merits. . . .

Constantius was industrious and had aspirations to learning, but he was too dull-witted to make a speaker, and when he turned his mind to versifying produced nothing worthwhile. His style of living was frugal and temperate, and he ate and

hordes that had penetrated across the middle and lower Danube. At that juncture, however, the offensive form of language employed by a party of German envoys so greatly angered him that he burst a blood vessel, with fatal results.

But he had left the western empire a good deal stronger than he found it eleven years earlier. No one could have believed that it only had a century of life ahead of it.

The Rise of Christian Intolerance

Three years later the other, eastern Roman empire experienced a catastrophic reverse. Beyond its frontiers, two German states had become established, the Ostrogoths ('bright Goths') in the Ukraine, and the Visigoths ('wise Goths') based in Rumania. The Ostrogothic group, however, crumbled before the cavalry onslaught of a non-German people, drank only in moderation; in consequence his health was so robust that he was rarely unwell. . . . In riding, throwing the javelin, and above all in archery, as well as in the various skills of the infantry, he was thoroughly expert. I will not dwell, because it has been related so often, on the fact that he was never seen in public wiping his face or nose or spitting or turning his head to either side and that he never in his life tasted fruit.

After picking out his good qualities, as far as I could ascertain them, I turn to the description of his defects. Although in most respects he was comparable with other emperors of average merit, yet if he discovered any ground, however false or slight, for suspecting an attempt upon the throne he showed in endless investigations, regardless of right or wrong, a cruelty which easily surpassed that of Caligula and Domitian and Commodus [earlier emperors known for their cruelty]. Indeed, at the very beginning of his reign he rivalled their barbarity by destroying root and branch all who were connected with him by blood and birth.

Ammianus Marcellinus, *History*, published as *The Later Roman Empire, A.D. 354–378*. Trans. and ed., Walter Hamilton. New York: Penguin Books, 1986, pp. 229–31.

the Huns (*c*.370), who also drove the Visigoths across the Danube into the eastern Roman provinces, where they were permitted to settle. But they were not treated fairly by Roman governmental officials, and their chief Fritigern, in disgust, rebelled and took over large areas of the Balkans. Valens marched from Asia to deal with the emergency, but perished in 378, in a battle at Hadrianopolis (Adrianople, Edirne), and the greater part of his army died with him. His nephew Gratian, the son and successor of Valentinian I in the west, had failed to reach the scene of the disaster in time to rescue his uncle. And now he appointed, as the dead man's successor, Theodosius I (378–395), an officer from Cauca (Coca) in Spain. Theodosius's personality veered abruptly between feverish activity and idleness. His rule, however, was notable in certain respects. First, he accepted a further, unprecedented mass of Visigothic settlers within his borders. And secondly, he insisted on strict Christian, Catholic orthodoxy, thus earning the title 'the Great'.

But the enforcement of this intention involved the rise of unmanageable churchmen. In particular, the reign of Theodosius witnessed the principal activity of Saint Ambrose (*c*.339–389). Ambrose was a new sort of Christian theologian, since he was not only a copious [prolific] writer and preacher but also showed himself a man of political authority and action. As bishop of Mediolanum (Milan), his aim was the creation of a wholly orthodox, Catholic, Christian empire, from which heresy and paganism and Judaism should all be eradicated. This was entirely in keeping with the ideas of Theodosius. However, Ambrose's actions also began to display resistance to the Constantinian doctrine that the Church should be subordinate to the state.

He had already shown his power when he persuaded Gratian's colleague in the west, Valentinian II (375–392), to reject the Roman aristocracy's pleas for the reerection of the Altar of Victory in the Senate house, a decision which inflicted a decisive blow upon paganism (384). But then he stood up to the more important eastern emperor, Theodosius I, as well. For in 390—when Theodosius was temporarily accessible to him in the west—Ambrose was bold enough to rebuke him publicly, and subject him to a penance, for having ordered a punitive massacre at Thessalonica (Salonica).

Toward a Divided Empire

But not all the leading cultural figures of the time were Christians. For example, Ambrose's principal opponent in the Altar of Victory controversy was the scholar, statesman and orator Symmachus, a supporter of the ancient pagan religion.

Moreover, Ammianus Marcellinus of Antioch (325/330–*c*.395), one of the most outstanding historians the empire ever produced, was also a pagan. After a military career, he wrote his *Roman History*, at Rome, during the later years of his life. The narrative, in Latin, covers the years from the accession of Nerva in AD 96 to the death of Valens in 378. Ammianus's account of the events of his own lifetime, in which he himself had participated, is particularly vivid. His determination to tell the truth is voiced with an insistence that is, on the whole, convincing. Yet, in the atmosphere of the later Roman spy state, it was impossible to write with candour about everybody—and the anti-Christian Ammianus stopped his history before the point when Theodosius I would have been discussed. Yet his admiration for the pagan Julian emerges, as does his approval of the tolerant, though Christian, policies of Valentinian I.

Displaying a gift not only for dramatic narrative but also for the depiction of character, Ammianus provides invaluable evidence for the declining years of the western empire: of which, over-optimistically, he did not foresee the imminent fall. He tends to under-estimate the Germans, but his treatment of the Persians is relatively unbiased.

After putting down two usurpers, Theodosius I succeeded in reuniting the eastern and western empires. But this reunification only proved momentary and transient, because after his death the two empires became divided once again, and this time division was permanent.

Chapter 2

The Disintegration of the Western Empire

Turning | Points

IN WORLD HISTORY

The Empire Is Permanently Divided

Arthur E.R. Boak and William G. Sinnegin

The period immediately following the death of the emperor Theodosius I in 395 was not only a violent, disruptive one for the western Empire, but also, to modern eyes, a confusing one. This is partly because dozens of different Germanic tribes, each with its own agenda, made their appearance in Roman lands. One moment they were fighting Romans, and the next they were joining the Romans against other Germans; while Roman leaders themselves frequently fought one another. All the while, various German tribes became federates (*foederati*), equal allies living within the Empire. Some of them eventually took the process a step further and set up independent kingdoms in former Roman provinces. Thus, the permanent division of the Empire came to include not only that between the western and eastern Roman spheres, but also the dismemberment and eventual loss of many important provinces, including those in Gaul, Britain, and Spain. The following admirable attempt to make sense of this complex and rapidly changing historical scene is by Arthur E.R. Boak, formerly of the University of Michigan, and William G. Sinnegin, formerly of Hunter College.

With the death of Theodosius the Great the Empire passed to his sons, Arcadius a youth of eighteen, whom he had left in Constantinople, and Honorius a boy of eleven, whom he had designated as Augustus for the West. However, in the East the government was really in the hands of Rufinus, the praetorian prefect of Illyricum, while an even greater influ-

Excerpted from *A History of Rome to 565 A.D.*, by E.R. Boak and William G. Sinnegin. Copyright ©1978. Reprinted by permission of Prentice-Hall, Inc., Upper Saddle River, NJ.

ence was exercised in the West by Stilicho, the Vandal master of the soldiers, whom Theodosius had selected as regent for young Honorius. The rivalry of these two ambitious men and the attempt by Stilicho to secure for Honorius restoration of eastern Illyricum, which had been seized by the eastern administration for Arcadius, were the immediate causes of the complete and formal division of the Empire into an eastern and a western half, a condition which had been foreshadowed by the division of imperial power throughout most of the fourth century.

The fiction of imperial unity was preserved by the nomination of one consul in Rome and one in Constantinople, by the joint display of the statues of both Augusti throughout the Empire, and by the issuance of imperial enactments under their joint names. There was, in fact, however, a complete separation of administrative authority. Before A.D. 395 edicts issued by one emperor required the sanction of the other before attaining validity within his own territory. After that date, the two parts of the Empire increasingly tended to separate legislatively, since edicts issued in one half were frequently not republished in the other. Furthermore, upon the death of one Augustus, the actual government of the whole Empire did not pass into his survivor's hands. The Empire had really split into two independent states.

In addition to the partition of the Empire, the period between 395 and 493 is marked by the complete breakdown of Roman resistance to barbarian invasion and the penetration and occupation of the western provinces and Italy by Germanic peoples. . . .

During this period of disintegration, the real power in the western Empire was in the hands of military dictators who, with the office of senior master of the soldiers, secured the position of commander in chief of the imperial armies and the title patrician. The emperors exercised only nominal authority. As these dictators were either barbarians or depended upon barbarian troops for their support, they were continually intrigued against and opposed by the Roman or civilian element, headed by the civil officers of the court. The fall of one "kingmaker" was always followed by the rise of another, for by their aid alone could the Romans offer any effective resistance to the flood of barbarian invasion.

But while the western Empire was thus absorbed by Germanic invaders, the East survived the crisis of the fifth century with its institutions and, generally speaking, its frontiers intact. This is in part accounted for by the ability of the central government in the East better to resist the decentralizing tendencies of the great landholders and of barbarian armies and their generals. In the West the greatest civil offices were held by members of the senatorial oligarchy, who encouraged the development of the vested economic interest of their own class and the spread of manorializing tendencies injurious to the imperial treasury. In the East, in contrast, important ministers of state were frequently civil servants of rather low social origin who, even if they were often corrupt, nevertheless owed a primary allegiance to the bureaucratic system that had produced them rather than to senatorial vested interest as such. The civil administration in the East held the army in check more effectively because of the division of supreme military authority among several masters of soldiers. The East also successfully solved the problem of barbarization of the army rank and file by purging it of barbarians on two notable occasions and by recruiting indigenous manpower from the Balkans, Asia Minor, and Armenia to take their place. The strength of the eastern Empire caused the West to come to look to it for support, and western emperors upon several occasions were nominated, and at other times given the sanction of legitimacy, by those in the East.

Barbarians Begin to Overrun the Western Provinces

Seizing the opportunity created by the death of Theodosius and the absence of the army of the East, which he had drawn into Italy, Alaric, a prince of the Visigothic *foederati*, began to ravage Thrace and Macedonia with a band of his own people, aided by other tribes from across the Danube. He was opposed by Stilicho, who was leading back the troops of the eastern emperor and intended to occupy eastern Illyricum. The latter was ordered by Arcadius to send the army of the East back to Constantinople, and he complied. This gave Alaric access to southern Greece, which he systematically plundered. Stilicho intervened again, transporting an army by sea to the Peloponnesus [the southern region of Greece]. He maneuvered Alaric into a precarious situation but came to terms with him, possibly because of a revolt that had broken out in Africa. Stilicho was declared an enemy by Arcadius, while Alaric, after devastating Epirus [in northwestern Greece], settled there with his Goths and extorted the title of *magister militum* from the eastern court.

In 401, when Stilicho was occupied with an inroad of Vandals and Alans into Raetia, Alaric invaded Italy. Stilicho forced him to withdraw and foiled a second attempt at invasion in 403. Alaric did not long remain inactive. He now held the title of master of the soldiers from Honorius and agreed to help Stilicho accomplish his designs upon Illyricum. When the western Empire was embarrassed by new invasions and the appearance of a usurper in Gaul, however, he made his way into Noricum, and demanded an indemnity [payment] and employment for his troops. On the advice of Stilicho his demands, which included a payment of 4,000 pounds of gold, were met. Shortly afterwards, Stilicho fell victim to a plot hatched by court officials who were jealous of his influence (408).

The death of Stilicho removed the only capable defender of Italy, and, when Honorius refused to honor the agreement with Alaric, the latter crossed the Alps. Honorius shut himself up in Ravenna, and the Goths marched on Rome, which was ransomed at a heavy price. As Honorius still refused to give him lands and supplies, Alaric returned to Rome and set up a new emperor, Attalus. Honorius, supported by troops from the eastern Empire, remained obdurate [stubborn], and a disagreement between Alaric and Attalus led to the latter's deposition. Rome was then occupied by the Goths, who plundered it for three days (410). Alaric's next move was to march to south Italy with the intention of crossing to Sicily and Africa, but his flotilla was destroyed by a storm. While retracing his steps northward he fell ill suddenly and died.

Alaric's successor was his brother-in-law, Ataulf, who led the Visigoths into Gaul (412), where he at first allied himself with a usurper, Jovinus, but soon deserted him to serve the Romans. When Honorius failed to furnish him supplies, he seized Narbonne and other towns in southern Gaul and married the emperor's sister, Galla Placidia, whom the Goths had captured in Rome. He again attempted to come to terms with the Romans but failed, and Constantius, the Roman master of the soldiers, who had succeeded to the position and influence of Stilicho, forced him to abandon Gaul. Ataulf and his Goths crossed the Pyrenees into Spain, where he died in 415. His successor Wallia, facing famine and failing in an attempt to invade Africa, came to terms with the Romans. He surrendered Placidia and in the name of the emperor attacked the Vandals and Alans who had occupied parts of Spain. Alarmed by his success, Constantius recalled the Goths to Gaul, where they were settled in southern Aquitania (418).

The status of the Goths in Gaul was that of *foederati*, bound to render military aid to Rome but governed by their own kings. The latter, however, had no authority over the Roman population among whom the Goths settled. This condition was unsatisfactory to the Gothic rulers, who sought to establish an independent Gothic kingdom. Theodoric I, the successor of Wallia, forced the Romans to acknowledge his complete sovereignty over Aquitania but failed in his attempt to conquer Narbonese Gaul. Subsequently he joined forces with the Romans against Attila the Hun and was largely responsible for checking the latter at the battle of the Mauriac plain near Troyes (451) in which he was killed. For a time the Goths remained on friendly terms with the Empire. Under Euric, who became king in 466, the anti-Roman faction was in the ascendant, and they embarked upon a policy of expansion. In 475 Euric, after a protracted struggle, occupied the district of Auvergne, and the Roman emperor acknowledged his sovereignty over the country between the Atlantic and the Rhone, the Loire, and the Pyrenees, besides some territory in Spain. Two years later the district between the Rhone and the Alps, South of the Durance, was added to the Visigothic kingdom.

Barbarians Against Barbarians

In 405 an invading band of Vandals and Alans had descended upon Italy, and were utterly defeated by Stilicho. In the following year fresh swarms of the same peoples, united with the Suevi, crossed the Rhine near Mainz and plundered Gaul as far as the Pyrenees. . . . Later . . . they found an opportunity to make their way into Spain (409).

They quickly made themselves masters of the whole Iberian peninsula. In spite of their successes against Roman troops, lack of supplies forced them to terms with the Empire. In 411 they became Roman *foederati* and were granted lands for settlement. Under this agreement the Asdingian Vandals and the Suevi occupied the northwest part of Spain, the Alans the center, and the Silingian Vandals the south. The Roman government made peace with the Vandals and their allies only under pressure and seized the first opportunity to be rid of these unwelcome guests. In 416 Constantius authorized the Visigoths under Wallia to attack them in the name of the emperor. Wallia was so successful that he utterly annihilated the Silingian Vandals and so weakened the Alans that they united with the Asdingian Vandals, who escaped destruction only through the recall of the Visigoths to Gaul. The Vandals quickly recovered from their defeats, waged successful war upon the Suevi, who had reached an agreement with the Romans, and occupied the whole of southern Spain.

In 429 the Vandals under their king Gaiseric crossed into Africa, attracted by its richness and its importance as one of the granaries of the Roman world. Their invasion was facilitated by war between Count Bonifacius, the military governor of Africa, and the western emperor. The number of the invaders was estimated at 80,000, of whom probably 15,000 or 20,000 were fighting men.

In spite of a reconciliation between Bonifacius and the imperial government and their united opposition, Gaiseric was able to overrun the open country, although he failed to capture the chief cities. In 435 peace was concluded, and the Vandals were allowed to settle in Numidia, once more as *foederati* of the Empire. . . .

Gaul and Britain Lost

The invasion of Gaul by the Vandals and Alans in 406 was followed by an inroad of the Burgundians, Ripuarian Franks, and Alamanni. The latter two peoples established themselves on the left bank of the Rhine, while the Burgundians penetrated farther south. In 433 the Burgundians were at war with the Empire and were defeated by Aetius, the Roman master of the soldiers in Gaul. Subsequently they were settled in Savoy. From there, about 457, they began to expand until they occupied the valley of the Rhone as far south as the Durance.

On the whole they remained loyal *foederati* of the Empire. They fought under Aetius against Attila in 451, and their kings bore the title of *magister militum* until the reign of Gundobad (473–516), who was given that of patrician by the emperor Olybrius.

The Salian Franks—as those who had once dwelt on the shores of the North Sea were called in contrast to the Ripuarians, whose home was along the Rhine—crossed the lower Rhine before 350 and occupied Toxandria, the region between the Meuse and the Scheldt. They were defeated by Julian, who left them in this district as *foederati*. The disturbances of the early fifth century enabled the Salian Franks to assert their independence and extend their territory as far south as the Somme. The fought as Roman allies against the Huns in 451, and their king Childeric, who began to rule shortly afterwards, remained a faithful *foederatus* until his death in 481.

In 486 Clovis, the successor of Childeric, overthrew the Gallo-Roman state south of the Somme and extended his kingdom to meet the Visigoths on the Loire. Thus the whole of Gaul passed under the rule of Germanic peoples.

After the decisive defeat of the Picts and Scots by Theodosius, father of Theodosius the Great, in 368 and 369, the Romans were able to maintain the defence of Britain until the close of the fourth century. In 402, however, Stilicho was obliged to recall part of the garrison for the protection of Italy, and in 406 Constantine, who claimed the imperial crown in Britain, took with him the remaining Roman troops in his attempt to obtain recognition on the continent. The ensuing struggles with the barbarians in Gaul prevented the Romans from sending officials or troops across the channel immediately, and the Britons for the time being had to fend for themselves.

The Roman garrison was eventually restored to the island . . . but it was unequal to stemming the tide of Saxons, Angles, and Jutes, who made permanent settlements beginning in 428. Toward 442 the Roman garrison evacuated the island forever. Four years later the inhabitants directed one last appeal to the Roman government for help, but it went unheeded. Because Roman civilization in Britain had been a relatively thin veneer, the subsequent struggle for possession of the island resulted in the obliteration of the Latin language and the disappearance of what material civilization had developed under four centuries of Roman rule.

Romans Against Romans

After the murder of Stilicho in 408, Honorius was faced with the problem of restoring his authority in Gaul, where for a time he was forced to acknowledge the rule of the rival emperor Constantine, who had donned the purple in Britain in 406. Constantius, a Roman noble who succeeded Stilicho as master of the soldiers, was dispatched to Gaul in 411 and soon overthrew the usurper. Two years later another rival, Jovinus, was crushed with the help of the Visigoths.

Constantius, leader of the antibarbarian faction of the court, was now the mainstay of Honorius' power and used his influence to further his own ambitions. After the Visigoths returned the princess Placidia, he induced the emperor to make her his wife (417). In 421 Honorius appointed him coemperor, but he was not recognized as an Augustus at Constantinople. His death the same year was followed by a quarrel between the emperor and his sister, as a result of which Placidia and her son took refuge with the eastern emperor, Theodosius II.

Honorius died in 423, leaving no children, and Castinus, the new commander in chief, secured the nomination of

John, a high officer of the court, as his successor. Theodosius refused him recognition, however, and his authority was defied by Bonifacius, an influential officer in Africa. Valentinian, the five-year-old son of Placidia and Constantius, was escorted to Italy by forces of the eastern Empire, and John was deposed. His chief supporter Aetius, who had brought an army of Huns to his aid, was induced to dismiss his troops and accept a command in Gaul with the rank of count. Placidia, who had returned to Italy with Valentinian, became regent with the title of Augusta.

During the reign of Valentinian III interest centered about the career of Aetius, "last of the Romans." In 429 . . . Aetius himself became master of the soldiers and the real ruler in the West. Fearing his influence, the Augusta Placidia endeavored to engineer his downfall by an appeal to Bonifacius, who, after his revolt of 427, had fought with the Empire against the Vandals. In 432 Bonifacius returned to Italy and was appointed master of the soldiers in place of Aetius. The latter took to arms, was defeated near Ariminum, and forced to flee to his friends the Huns. Bonifacius died not long after his victory; Aetius, with the backing of the Huns, was able to force the emperor to reappoint him to his command as patrician in 433. From that time until his death in 454 he directed imperial policy in the West. He received embassies from foreign peoples, and the latter made treaties with him and not with the emperor.

The chief efforts of Aetius were directed toward the preservation of central and southeastern Gaul for the Empire. In this he was successful, holding in check the Franks on the north, the Burgundians on the east, and the Goths in the southwest. Gaul was saved, but Africa was lost to the Vandals, Britain to the Saxons, and the greater part of Spain to the Suevi. The success of Aetius in Gaul was due principally to his ability to draw on large numbers of Hunnish troops, through the influence he had acquired with the leaders of that people while a hostage among them. At this time the Huns occupied the region of modern Hungary, Rumania, and South Russia. They comprised many separate tribes, which were united in 444 under the strong hand of King Attila, who extended his sway over neighboring Germanic and Scythian peoples.

At first Attila remained on friendly terms with Aetius, but his ambitions and his interference in Gaul led to friction and to his demand for the hand of Honoria, sister of Valentinian III, with half of the western Empire as her dowry. When the emperor refused to comply, Attila led a great army across the Rhine into Gaul and besieged Orleans.

The Huns Terrorize Europe

Stewart Perowne

In a very real sense, the Huns, who originated in central Asia, did more to bring down the western Roman realm than any other single "barbarian" people. This was because their initial onslaught, in the 370s, set in motion the major folk migrations that ultimately overran the Empire. Later, under their fearsome war leader Attila, the Huns also came perilously close to sacking Rome. This able summary of Attila, his talents, aims, methods, and attacks on the Empire is by the late English historian Stewart Perowne, who specialized in the Later Empire.

The Huns . . . owe their retrospective reputation to one outstanding and extraordinary man, Attila, and to the fact that we have a more intimate picture of him and of his court than of any other barbarian chieftain. To start with, Ammianus has told us a good deal about the Huns, of their unimaginable ferocity, their squat bodies, their great arms and shoulders, slit eyes and flat noses. Their checks were scarified in infancy to prevent the growth of hair. They ate raw flesh. They never changed their clothes. They stank. They lived all their days on horseback, their nights too, sleeping along the necks of their mounts. They were completely nomadic, these terrible little yellow men, and hauled their women and children behind them in wagons.

Born to Strike Terror

This description alone would be enough to set the Huns apart from other men, even barbarians, in popular estimation; but it so happens that we have an even closer view of Attila and his court on the Hungarian steppe, from the pen of a

Greek with a Roman name, Priscus, who accompanied an embassy from the Byzantine court to Attila in the year 449. He has left us a narrative which in its detail, balance and colour recalls the best productions of the journalism of travel of the nineteenth century, when that form of literature was in its hey-day. There is the long journey, the meeting with the envoys of the Huns, the first suspicious contacts, misunderstandings, explanations, resentments, the tactless remarks construed as insults—the scene has been re-enacted countless times when Europeans and Asians have assembled to discuss a possible accommodation. Then comes the long trek to Attila's court, secure beyond its five days' journey of scorched earth on the north bank of the Danube. The visitors wanted to pitch their tents *en route* on a hill, but that would have offended the majesty of their host, who assigned them a site on the plain where his own encampment was spread.

Attila's dwelling in Hungary was splendid. It was one great hall made of beautifully compacted wood, fenced round with a wooden palisade. It was sumptuously furnished with rich carpets and tapestries. Gold, silks and gems abounded. There was a bath, on the Roman plan, supervised by a Greek. It was constructed of imported stone. There were banquets, at which the food was choice and the wine delicious. Minstrels and jesters entertained the guests during dinner, girls were there to solace them afterwards—a customary attention, says Priscus, which he modestly declined. Costly gifts were exchanged.

In the midst of all the splendour Attila sat stern, unsmiling and austere. While the guests ate off gold plates and drank from jewelled goblets, Attila ate frugally from a wooden platter and drank from a cup of the same material. "This man," says [the sixth-century Gothic writer] Jordanes, "aspired to conquer the two greatest powers on earth, the Romans and the Visigoths. His army, they say, numbered half a million. He was born into this world in order to shake his own people, and to strike terror into everyone. By some stroke of fate, the fear he inspired seemed to spread ahead of him. He had a proud gait, darting his eyes this way and that, and his pride of power shewed itself in the way he moved.

He loved war, but kept a hold of himself when in action. He was an excellent councillor, and always accessible to petitioners, and kind to those he had received into his protection. He was short of stature, with a broad chest and a strong head. He had little eyes, a scanty beard streaked with gray, a snub nose and a darkish skin. In fact he was absolutely typical of his race."

Attila Threatens the East

Except in one regard. For generations Huns had enlisted in the Roman army. Stilicho the Vandal had raised a whole regiment of them, so had Honorius. Attila himself had served in the imperial forces; he also provided many recruits for the Roman army. Then, about the year 430, Attila realized that the empire was no longer a lion to be feared, but a cow to be milked.

He decided that he, not Rome, was to be master of the world. Like Alaric before him, he made his first essays against the eastern empire. His policy was simple: it was to alternate violence with blackmail. In the year 440 Rome was in sore straits. The year before, Carthage had fallen to the Vandals, which meant not only the loss of one of the empire's most abundant granaries but also that a hostile fleet based on Carthage could menace the eastern no less than the western dominions of Rome.

By a crippling coincidence, the Persians had chosen this very year to invade Roman Armenia, on what pretext is not known. The northern frontier was thus left almost bare. Attila saw that his chance had come, and decided to strike.

He crossed the Danube. Viminacium (modern Kostolacz), one of the major strong-points of the Roman *limes* [borders], was captured and razed to the ground. So was Singidunum (Belgrade). Worst of all, Sirmium, the very key to the whole of the Danube defence system, fell to Attila. The Balkans lay open to him, but, content with his booty and his captives, he undertook no campaign in the following year. He preferred to treat with Rome. The Hun was now insistent that all of his tribesmen in Roman pay should be handed back to him—this demand was to recur in all his many negotiations with Rome.

Ammianus on the Huns

In this excerpt from his history of Rome, Ammianus provides price-less details about the appearance, personal habits, and fighting style of the Huns.

The people of the Huns, who are mentioned only cursorily in ancient writers and who dwell beyond the Sea of Azov [north of the Black Sea] near the frozen ocean, are quite abnormally savage. From the moment of birth they make deep gashes in their children's cheeks, so that when in due course hair appears its growth is checked by the wrinkled scars; as they grow older this gives them the unlovely appearance of beardless eunuchs. They have squat bodies, strong limbs, and thick necks, and are so prodigiously ugly and bent that they might be two-legged animals, or the figures crudely carved from stumps which are seen on the parapets of bridges. Still, their shape, however disagreeable, is human; but their way of life is so rough that they have no use for fire or seasoned food, but live on the roots of wild plants and the half-raw flesh of any sort of animal, which they warm a little by placing it between their thighs and the backs of their horses. They have no buildings to shelter them, but avoid anything of the kind as carefully as we avoid living in the neighbourhood of tombs; not so much as a hut thatched with reeds is to be found among them. They roam at large over mountains and forests, and

Henceforth, any Hun who took service in the Roman ranks was regarded as a traitor, who, if he were handed back, risked crucifixion or impalement. In 443 Attila renewed his offensive. Nish, the birthplace of Constantine, was captured and destroyed, and the Huns then swept down to the sea, which they reached at three different points. They approached Constantinople itself, but were too prudent to attack it. Nevertheless, Theodosius [II, reigned 408–450] was forced to beg for terms. The barbarian exacted from the empire not only the return of the fugitives but arrears of tribute as well—Constantinople had been paying it for the past eight years—calculated at 6,000 pounds of gold. In addition, the sum payable under the treaty of 435 was to be trebled, which are inured from the cradle to cold, hunger, and thirst. . . . They wear garments of linen or of the skins of field-mice stitched together, and there is no difference between their clothing whether they are at home or abroad. Once they have put their necks into some dingy shirt they never take it off or change it till it rots and falls to pieces from incessant wear. They have round caps of fur on their heads, and protect their hairy legs with goatskins. . . .

They sometimes fight *by challenging their foes to single combat*, but when they join battle they advance in packs, uttering their various war cries. Being lightly equipped and very sudden in their movements they can deliberately scatter and gallop about at random, inflicting tremendous slaughter; their extreme nimbleness enables them to force a rampart or pillage an enemy's camp before one catches sight of them. What makes them the most formidable of all warriors is that they shoot from a distance arrows tipped with sharp splinters of bone instead of the usual heads; these are joined to the shafts with wonderful skill. At close quarters they fight without regard for their lives, and while their opponents are guarding against sword-thrusts they catch their limbs in lassos of twisted cloth which make it impossible for them to ride or walk.

Ammianus Marcellinus, *History*, published as *The Later Roman Empire*, A.D. 354–378. Trans. and ed., Walter Hamilton. New York: Penguin Books, 1986, pp. 411–12.

meant that Attila was to receive 2,000 pounds of gold each year. Roman prisoners who escaped from their Hun captors were to be ransomed at the rate of twelve *solidi* a head, in place of the eight formerly stipulated.

The embassy which arranged these humiliating provisions was followed by four more, in quick succession. Attila's object was simply to collect as often as possible the handsome presents which Theodosius felt constrained to give to his emissaries: he was as versatile in levying blackmail as he was resolute in war.

In 447 Attila again invaded the eastern empire, enfeebled once more by a series of destructive earthquakes, followed by plague. Not less than seventy towns were destroyed, and the invasion was checked only at Thermopylae [in central Greece]. The next years were once again, in accordance with Attila's policy, devoted to negotiations, and it was in 449 that Priscus accompanied an embassy to Attila as already related. The same old subjects were discussed, the return of fugitives, the ransoming of prisoners; and a deputation from the west was there, too, to debate the apparently rather trivial matter of certain church plate from Sirmium, which Attila claimed was his by right of conquest, but which had in fact been taken to Rome and there pawned. The outcome we do not know.

Attila Turns on the West

Attila now decided that the time had come for him to turn against the west. One of the reasons he had hitherto held his hand was his friendship with Aëtius, the western commander-in-chief, who had been a hostage in the hands of the Huns as a boy, and still cultivated Attila's friendship. In fact, Attila was actually given the rank of *magister militum* of the western empire. It was not intended that he should command Roman troops; but the rank carried a good salary, and a liberal grain allowance. It was, in fact, a decorous and delicate instrument of bribery.

Attila's onslaught upon the west was to be launched through a woman. Galla Placidia [half-sister of the emperor Honorius] had a daughter called Honoria. Like her mother, she was romantic. In the year 449 she was thirty-two, but alas! still unmarried. She allowed herself to be seduced by one of her gentlemen. The intrigue was discovered, the lover executed and Honoria engaged to a dull, rich senator. This was too much—or rather far too little—for Honoria. If her mother had married a barbarian king, why should not she? In the spring of 450 she sent a letter and a ring to Attila by a eunuch called Hyacinth, asking him, in return for a cash consideration, to rescue her from an impossible marriage.

Poor Honoria's plan was frustrated: Valentinian handed her over to Galla Placidia, who died soon afterwards, to be buried perhaps in the splendid tomb in Ravenna which she had done so little to deserve. What happened to Honoria we do not know; but Attila claimed her as his bride and half the western empire as her dowry. Gaiseric the Vandal, by far the subtlest manipulator of the century, urged him to press his claim.

In 451 Attila attacked. He crossed the Rhine, seized several French towns (though not as many as legend afterwards pretended) and on 23rd June had forced Orléans to surrender, when suddenly Aëtius appeared and put the besiegers to flight. At the head of his mongrel but disciplined army, Aëtius pursued the Huns and defeated them at the famous battle of the Catalaunian Fields (it was actually fought near Troyes) at the end of August. Europe, the as yet unborn Europe, was saved on that day.

End of the Hun Menace

Aëtius did not follow up his victory: he was thinking of the balance of power, and had no desire to aggrandize [increase the power of] the Visigoths, whom he had induced to fight as his allies against his old friend. Next year, therefore, Attila was still able to mount a campaign. He again approached Italy, and seized the hitherto inviolable [safe from violation] fortress of Aquileia. His European advisers, the Roman Orestes and the Greek Onegeses, advised him to move on Rome—of which Orestes' own son was to be the last emperor. Attila was just about to cross the Mincio [River], when he was confronted by a solemn procession, chanting hymns and headed by no less a person than Pope Leo himself. No one knows what the two men said to each other. On his return all that Leo would say to Valentinian was: "Let us give thanks to God for he has delivered us from great danger." The incident had vast echoes: it shewed that, despite all the pagans might say, it was the Church which prevailed where they did not.

Within the year Attila, who had retired on the promise of a tribute, was dead: marriage at the age of nearly seventy to a lusty young German girl had proved too much for the man who had ravished half Europe. He was found in a fit on the bridal bed.

With Attila, so rapid can be the changes of the kaleidoscope, the Hun menace, too, was extinct.

The Vandals Sack Rome

Justine D. Randers-Pehrson

With numerous barbarian groups roaming the Empire in search of new lands, it was only a matter of time before some of them threatened Rome itself. Though no longer the capital of the western Empire (the royal court was now in the Italian town of Ravenna), it was still the symbol of over a thousand years of Roman tradition and glory. Alaric the Visigoth had occupied Rome in 410, but had stayed only three days and done little damage. In the years that followed, however, the Vandals, under their dedicated leader Gaiseric, posed a new threat to the Empire. In this excerpt from her widely acclaimed book, *Barbarians and Romans*, scholar Justine D. Randers-Pehrson draws on the works of the sixth-century Gothic writer Jordanes, the sixth-century Byzantine historian Procopius, and other contemporary sources to tell how the Vandals came to sack Rome in 455. She begins much earlier, with their perilous trek through Spain, the Suevi, Visigoths, and other groups threatening their rear; their crossing into Africa and establishment of a kingdom there; and their dealings with Roman leaders, including the formidable general Aëtius, often called "the last of the Romans."

In spite of their unappetizing reputation, the Vandals did not spend their entire lives ravaging the civilized world. The term "vandalism," which has become attached to acts of wanton destructiveness, has nothing to do with them. It was coined by Bishop Grégoire of Blois, who was talking about the French Revolution, not about the struggles of wandering folk in the time of the great migrations.

Before landing in Africa, the Vandals had suffered many

Excerpted from *Barbarians and Romans: The Birth Struggle of Europe, A.D. 400–700*, by Justine Davis Randers-Pehrson. Copyright ©1983 by Justine Davis Randers-Pehrson. Reprinted with permission from the University of Oklahoma Press.

trials in Spain. Romanized provincials were there, ready prey for their raids, but the Suevi had come along too, and relationships with those people were not smooth. At their backs the Vandals had their traditional enemies the Visigoths, then commissioned by Ravenna to control if not exterminate them. As targets of Constantius's intricate policies, the Vandals, the Alans, and the Suevi jostled about in their cul-de-sac, and conditions were difficult indeed. Immediately after Constantius's death General Castinus was sent to Spain, in command of a large force directed against them. Although the Vandals routed Castinus, they were still menaced by the Visigoths, and they knew that Ravenna could be expected to pounce again someday. The triumph over Castinus may have served as a signal to the Vandals that at that moment the empire was unusually weak.

The Trek into Africa

They beat back the Suevi in a savage engagement and then turned their attention to the logistics of crossing water, all eighty thousand of them. Most figures indicating the numbers of barbarian hordes are unreliable, coming from the fevered minds of Romans who saw twenty barbarians where actually there was one, but this time the count must have been more trustworthy than usual. There had to be an accurate determination of the number of vessels needed for the crossing to Africa.

How would one go about transporting eighty thousand individuals with their horses, livestock, and household gear across a strait some fifteen centuries ago? . . . They must have taken the shortest possible route, near Gibraltar, shuttled across by small fishing craft. The operation rather recalls the rescue of the British army from Dunkirk in 1940. Two or three men handling a small boat could ferry four or five Vandals and their gear, negotiating a sixty-two-kilometer round trip in twenty-four hours. If there were five hundred fishing boats, which is not beyond possibility, the Vandals and Alans could have arrived in force on the beaches east of modern Tangiers by the end of thirty-two laborious days.

Did "a huge host of savage enemies armed with every kind

of weapon" actually swarm all over Mauretania and the African provinces, as Possidius reports in his biography of Saint Augustine? . . .

[In reality] it took them a full three months to travel seven hundred kilometers. Women and children and the aged could not move along at an efficient pace, and the host had to fan out into foraging parties to sustain itself. Seven months were required to negotiate the next twelve hundred kilometers. Gaiseric and his people arrived before Hippo in May or June, 430, just months before the death of Augustine. . . .

Gaiseric had an acute sense of timing. His shift from Spain to Africa followed the defeat of Castinus, and his next major move was triggered apparently by a Roman defeat at Toulouse. He immediately . . . moved on to Carthage, which he was able to enter without striking a blow on October 19, 439. . . .

The regnal years [royal reigns] of the Vandal kings date from the capitulation of Carthage. Gaiseric was much more kingly there than he had been as chieftain of a wandering host. Double kingship had been characteristic of the Vandals in Europe, but Gaiseric ruled alone. Ancient traditions were discarded: gone was the tribal council. This is our first chance to see what happens when a barbarian kingdom becomes established on Roman soil. In the initial stages we know that there will be violence, unrest, cruelty, and sorrow, but we anticipate something exciting to result from the novel arrangement. . . .

Vandal Rule in Africa

The Vandals ruled Africa for a century. Even by the time of the dispersal there had been astonishingly few changes. The period of Vandal domination was not dull and flat, but it might have had a more vivid tone.

Gaiseric was the dominant figure. This man had a fearsomely cunning intelligence, with an uncanny comprehension of emerging political forces. Procopius refers to him as the cleverest of all men. According to Jordanes, "He was a man of deep thought and few words, holding luxury in disdain, furious in his anger, shrewd in winning over the barbarians and skilled in sowing the seeds of dissension." It is odd that in popular estimation he has been so overshadowed by his Hunnic contemporary Attila, because he was infinitely more adroit. Moreover, the aftereffects of his manipulation of the strands that were supposed to bind the empire together were much more enduring than those of Attila in his brief appearance on the European stage.

Unfortunately, Gaiseric had no more comprehension of what a new world order might be than did any of his adversaries overseas. His thought was so concentrated on the narrow problem of security for his people and the filling of their hungry mouths that not once did he look about him to assess the potentialities of the complex administrative tools that he had seized from Rome. The apparatus offered no challenge to his mind. His duty was exclusively that of the tribal chieftain, centered on the distribution of booty that included whole fertile farms and estates, not just the usual captured flocks and occasional troves of coin and tableware. . . .

The most interesting aspect of Vandal rule, especially under Gaiseric, was the entrance of this new, untried kingdom into the complex world of diplomacy. The first venture was an obvious one. Gaiseric engineered a lasting agreement of some kind with the powerful general Aspar, who, in all his years as the dominant figure at the court of Constantinople, had never made so much as a gesture against the Vandals. As we observed before, Aspar was an Alan, and Gaiseric had assumed the title *rex Alanorum*. There were, however, other moves on the diplomatic front that were more subtle and showed some grasp of the principle of the balance of powers. Gaiseric's problem lay in the circumstance that he had two enemies across the sea, namely the Romans and the Visigoths. His first move was to accept the daughter of the king of the Visigoths as a wife for his son Huneric, thus establishing a somewhat wavering alliance between the two previously hostile nations. . . .

In the year 442 a pact had been drawn up acknowledging Gaiseric's legal claim to Carthage. Romans and Vandals became allies. The West recovered the more barren and remote parts of Africa in return for this recognition. It must have been in the year of the pact or shortly thereafter that Emperor Valentinian III formally betrothed his daughter Eudocia, who was about five years old, to Gaiseric's son Huneric, who was already married to a Visigoth princess. . . .

Who could have proposed it, and why? It could be argued that Aëtius saw that the best policy for keeping Gaiseric in check would be to cultivate good relations with him. That would remove any pretext for [a Vandal] attack on Sardinia or Sicily or even on Italy itself. Aëtius would want to keep Vandal-Visigoth enmity alive. On the other hand, it is not even certain that Aëtius had much to do with the treaty of 442, let alone with Eudocia's engagement to Huneric. Such a marriage might be a personal threat to Aëtius, in view of his own ambitions (he demanded that Valentinian's younger daughter Placidia be given to his son Gaudentius). Possibly the emperor would have found the marital alliance with the house of Gaiseric to his own liking, as a means for counterbalancing the influence of Aëtius. Let him call in his Huns: he, Valentinian, could then summon Vandals. Either way Gaiseric would gain. He could be reasonably sure that no serious effort would be made to dislodge him from Africa. . . .

Rome at Gaiseric's Mercy

[But in the next thirteen years, the situation changed dramatically.] Whether or not Gaiseric's activities had actually set in motion the train of dramatic events, the outcome was in his favor. In Gaul the Visigoths were in some disorder. So were the Huns, and so was the Western empire. Theodoric the Visigoth was dead. Attila [leader of the Huns] was dead. Aëtius was dead. Valentinian III, the last of the Theodosian dynasty, was dead. The new emperor, Petronius Maximus, had been implicated in the murder of Valentinian. To secure his shaky hold on his new office, he forced himself as husband on Valentinian's widow, Eudoxia, and also speedily arranged another highly injudicious marriage, that of his son to Valentinian's daughter Eudocia, the girl who had been engaged for so long to Gaiseric's son Huneric. This was a gratuitous insult to the Vandal king. . . . The situation was a barbarian's dream come true.

When Emperor Maximus learned that Gaiseric's fleet was heading across the sea, he tried to make his escape, but a raging mob cut him down. Gaiseric and his Vandals along with Moorish troops appeared at the gates of Rome in May, 455. Once again majestic Pope Leo [who had persuaded Attila not to sack Rome] valiantly confronted a barbarian invader, but this one was not to be deflected. Gaiseric agreed not to put the noble city to the torch and not to permit a general massacre, but that was the sum of his concessions. Prisoners were taken by the thousands, including many young persons and artisans, especially those skilled in making weapons. Important political prisoners were also taken, among them Aëtius's son Gaudentius, the empress, and her two daughters. Eudocia at last became Huneric's wife. . . .

For two weeks the Vandals methodically sought out and stowed onto their ships everything portable and precious still to be found in public and private Rome—everything from jewels to gilded roofing materials. After this it would not be possible to speak of the city's metallic luster that Prudentius and Claudian praised. Today there must still be a sprawl of statues, cargo that sank on the way to Carthage, lying on the floor of the Mediterranean.

A few things here and there escaped. Pope Leo is said to have been required to surrender gleaming golden altar vessels with his own hands, but he managed to salvage some gigantic silver urns that had been gifts of Constantine the Great. At a later time he had them melted down to furnish the bare altars of robbed Roman churches with simpler vessels.

For the third time tremulous Rome lay helpless before a barbarian. Like Alaric and Attila before him, Gaiseric seems to have had no thought of establishing himself there as a permanent ruler, though in the year 455 he was certainly the most powerful man in the Western world. Alaric was driven on in search of food for his hungry host, while Attila was turned back by an epidemic and possibly also by superstitious fear of Rome the Eternal. What about Gaiseric? He knew that no barbarian should ever wear the imperial purple, but he was not a man to be swayed by custom. Perhaps even Gaiseric felt awe before timeless Rome. He withdrew to Carthage, content to carry on as before with his booty and his power to threaten anyone whose land edged the Mediterranean, including the Adriatic.

The Last Western Roman Emperors

J.B. Bury

In 455, after the emperor Valentinian III was murdered in retaliation for his own killing of the popular general Aëtius, and the Vandals sacked Rome, western Rome's political deterioration accelerated. Another general, Ricimer, set up a number of what were in effect puppet emperors who all recognized that he held the real power. Then, after he died, still another powerful military man, the German-born Odovacar (or Odoacer), rose to prominence; and it was he who deposed the last western Roman emperor, Romulus Augustulus. As the late distinguished classical historian J.B. Bury explains here, technically speaking another imperial claimant, Julius Nepos, was still recognized as the legitimate western ruler by the eastern Roman court. But Nepos died before he could press his claim. Bury also points out that at the time no one viewed these events as catastrophic or fancied that the western Empire had collapsed; for Odovacar and other Germans continued to administer a very much intact Rome. The idea of the year 476 being a great historical turning point did not become fashionable until much later.

The forty years succeeding the collapse of the Empire of the Huns, from about 454 to 493, were marked by the gradual advance of the German power in Gaul and Spain; while before 493 Italy itself had become a German kingdom. Now the steady increase of the barbarian power, and the steady decline of the imperial power, in the west during these years was largely conditioned . . . by the existence and hostility of

Excerpted from *Invasion of Europe by the Barbarians*, by J.B. Bury. Reprinted by permission of Macmillan Press, Ltd.

the Vandal power in north Africa. The Vandal king Gaiseric had formed a strong fleet with which he was able to attack and plunder Italy, as well as to occupy Sicily and Sardinia. . . . The presence of this enemy in Africa . . . immeasurably weakened the Roman power in all the western provinces. It had the direct result of controlling the corn supply of Italy, and it prevented the Roman government from acting with effectual vigour in either Gaul or Spain. If the Romans had continued to hold Africa—if the Vandals had not been there—there can be little doubt that the imperial power would have maintained itself for a far longer period in Italy, and would have offered far more effective opposition to the expansion of the Germans in Gaul and Spain. In my view, therefore, the contribution which the Vandals made to the shaping of Europe was this: the very existence of their kingdom in Africa, and of their naval power in the Mediterranean, acted as a powerful protection for the growth of the new German kingdoms in Gaul and Spain, and ultimately helped the founding of a German kingdom in Italy, by dividing, diverting, and weakening the forces of the Empire. The Vandals had got round, as it were, to the rear of the Empire; and the effect of their powerful presence there was enhanced by the hostile and aggressive attitude which they continuously adopted.

Ricimer the German

Even if there had been united councils in Italy, the task of ubiquitous defence would have been beyond the power of the government; but the government went to pieces, and thereby hastened the dismemberment [of the realm]. I need not here enter at all into the history of the short-reigned emperors who were set up and knocked down in Italy after the murder of Valentinian III in 455. I would invite your attention to two main points: first, the Vandal danger which embarrassed the Italian government during these years; and secondly, the power behind the imperial throne. This power behind the throne is of great significance. . . . It was wielded by a German general, Ricimer, of Suevian race. He was the successor of the German Stilicho and of the Roman Aetius as the defender of the Empire. The circumstances in which Ricimer had to act were indeed different from the circumstances of Stilicho and of Aetius. They differed in two main particulars. First, . . . while the activity of Stilicho and of Aetius reached beyond Italy to the other western provinces, the activity of Ricimer was practically confined to Italy and the Italian seas: this was due to the powerful hostility of the Vandals. Secondly, Stilicho and Aetius had been the ministers of emperors who belonged to the well-established dynasty of Theodosius; and although those emperors, Honorius and Valentinian III, were personally weak and worthless, yet their legitimacy gave their thrones stability; so that Stilicho and Aetius could feel that, though they might fall themselves, they had a secure throne behind them. It was not so in the case of Ricimer. The male line of Theodosius was extinct; Valentinian III had left no sons: and it devolved upon Ricimer to provide the imperial authority which he was to serve. He became through circumstances an emperor-maker; and his difficulty was this. If he set up too strong a man, his own power would have probably been overridden; his own fall would have been the consequence; while on the other hand weak upstarts were unable to maintain their position for any length of time, since public opinion did not respect them. In estimating the part played by Ricimer, I think that hard and unjust measure is sometimes dealt out to him. The difficulties of his position can hardly be over-stated, and he may be held to have made a serious and honest attempt to perform the task of preserving a government in Italy and defending the peninsula against its formidable enemies.

Now you must observe that the fact of Ricimer's being a German was a significant and determining factor in the situation. If he had not been a German, the situation would have been much simpler; for he could have assumed the imperial purple himself; the real and the nominal power would have been combined in the same hands; and the problem of government would have been solved. His German birth excluded this solution. This is a very remarkable thing. Germans like Stilicho and Ricimer, who attained to the highest posts in the imperial service, who might even intermarry with the imperial house, could not venture to take the last great step and mount the imperial throne. Just so much, just at the pinnacle, they were still outsiders. And they fully recognised this disability themselves. . . .

Enter Nepos and Orestes

It is also to be noted that in the intervals between the reigns of the emperors whom Ricimer set up and pulled down, when there was no emperor regnant [ruling] in Italy, it did not mean that there was no emperor at all. At such times the imperial authority was entirely invested in the eastern emperor who reigned at Constantinople, the Emperor Leo; and this, too, was fully acknowledged by Ricimer, who indeed selected two of his emperors by arrangement with Leo.

Ricimer died in 472 and the march of affairs after his death shows how difficult his task had been. The events of these next few years have often been misconceived in respect of the exact nature of their importance. Ricimer's nephew Gundobad seemed marked out to succeed to the place of his uncle—as the head of the military forces in Italy, and as the power behind the throne. Gundobad belonged to the royal family of the Burgundians and was a son of the reigning Burgundian king; but he had entered the imperial service. The Emperor Olybrius, Ricimer's last creation, recognised Gundobad's position and raised him to the rank of patrician. But Olybrius died before the end of the year, and a crisis ensued. For Gundobad and the Emperor Leo could not agree as to who should succeed to the purple. Leo's candidate was Julius Nepos, and Gundobad set up an obscure person named Glycerius. . . .

But hardly had the deadlock arisen between Gundobad and the Emperor Leo, when Gundobad disappeared from the scene. A new ambition was suddenly opened to him. . . . His father had died, and Gundobad withdrew to Burgundy to endeavour to secure his own election [to the Burgundian throne]. He succeeded. . . . After his departure the Emperor Julius Nepos, Leo's candidate, landed in Italy and deposed Glycerius. But Nepos was not equal to the situation. He very wisely negotiated a peace with Euric, king of the West Goths,

. . . and he then appointed a certain Roman, Orestes by name, to be commander-in-chief, *magister militum*, in Gaul, to defend the Roman territory there. Orestes had been in Attila's service: he had lived much with barbarians of all kinds, and Nepos thought that he was making a very clever choice in selecting Orestes to command an army of barbarian soldiers. I may point out that after the break-up of Attila's empire there had been an immense influx of barbarian mercenaries into the Roman service. The army which Orestes now commanded was composed not only of Germans drawn from families long settled in the Empire but also of these new adventurers who had drifted into Italy through Noricum and Pannonia. Nepos was deceived in Orestes; Orestes was ambitious, and instead of going to Gaul, as he had been told, he marched on Ravenna. Nepos immediately fled to Dalmatia. Italy was for the moment in the power of Orestes. He did not seize the Empire himself, he preferred the double arrangement which had prevailed in the time of Ricimer. . . . Keeping the military power himself, he invested his child-son Romulus Augustulus with the imperial purple.

Rise of Odovacar

But before Orestes had established his government he was surprised by a new situation. His host of barbarian soldiers, who were largely Heruls, suddenly formulated a demand. They were dissatisfied with the arrangements for quartering them. Their wives and children lived in the garrison towns in their neighbourhood, but they had no proper homes or hearths. The idea occurred to them that arrangements might be made in their behalf in Italy similar to those which had been made in Gaul, for instance, in behalf of the Visigoths and the Burgundians. Why should not they obtain permanent quarters, abiding homes, on the large estates . . . of Italy? This feeling prevailed in the host, and the officers formulated a demand which they laid before Orestes. The demand simply was that the normal system of *hospitalitas* should be adopted in Italy for their benefit, *i.e.* that a third part of the Italian soil should be divided among them. The sympathies or prejudices of Orestes were too Roman to let him entertain this demand; Italy had so far been sacrosanct [safe] from barbarian settlements. He refused, and his refusal led to a revolution. The mercenary soldiers found a leader in an officer who was thoroughly representative of themselves, an adventurer who had come from beyond the Danube to seek his fortunes, and had entered the service of the Empire. This was Odovacar: he was probably a Scirian, possibly a Rugian (there is a discrepancy in the authorities), at all events he . . . now undertook to realise the claim of the soldiers, and consequently there was a revolution. Orestes was put to death, and his son the Emperor Romulus Augustulus abdicated. The power in Italy was in the hands of Odovacar. We are in the year 476.

Odovacar Negotiates with Constantinople

There was, constitutionally speaking, nothing novel in the situation. There were two legitimate emperors, the Emperor Zeno at Constantinople, and the Emperor Julius Nepos (who was in Dalmatia). In the eyes of the government of Constantinople, Romulus Augustulus was a usurper. This usurper had now been deposed by a military revolution; the leader of that revolution, Odovacar, had shown no disloyalty to the eastern emperor, whose authority he fully acknowledged. There was no thought here of any dismemberment, or detachment, or breaking away from the Empire. Odovacar was a Roman officer, he was raised by the army into the virtual position of a *magister militum*, and his first thought, after the revolution had been carried through, was to get his position regularised by imperial authority, to gain from Zeno a formal recognition and appointment. Odovacar was in fact the successor of the series of German commanders who had supported the Empire for eighty years: and when he came to power in 476, there was not the least reason in the actual circumstances why the same kind of regime should not have been continued as in the days of Ricimer. But Odovacar had statesmanlike qualities, and he decided against the system of Ricimer, which had proved thoroughly unsatisfactory and unstable. His idea was to rule Italy under the imperial authority of Constantinople, unhampered by a second emperor in Italy, whom recent experiences had shown to be worse than useless. There would have been no difficulty for Odovacar in adopting this policy, if there had existed no second emperor at the time; but Julius Nepos was still alive, and, what was most important, he had been recognised at Constantinople. Odovacar was determined *not* to acknowledge the authority of Nepos. It is very important to understand this element in the situation, because it directly led to the peculiar position which Odovacar afterwards occupied. He first addressed himself to the Roman senate, and caused that body to send envoys to Constantinople, bearing the imperial insignia, and a letter to the Emperor Zeno. The purport of the letter was to suggest that one emperor, namely Zeno himself and his successors at Constantinople, sufficed for the needs of the whole Empire, and to ask that Zeno should authorise Odovacar to conduct the administration in Italy, and should confer on him the title of Patricius, which had been borne by Ricimer. The Emperor was not a little embarrassed. Julius Nepos was at the same time demanding his help to recover Italy, and Nepos had a legitimate claim. The Emperor wrote a very diplomatic reply. He insisted, in the most definite and correct terms, on the legal claim of Nepos; he, however, told Odovacar, whom he praised for the consideration he had shown in his dealings with the Italians after the revolution, that he would confer upon him the title of Patricius, if Nepos had not already done so.

Odovacar's Revolution

This limited recognition was not what Odovacar had hoped for; the express reserve of the rights of Julius Nepos was most unsatisfactory; there was always a chance that those rights might at a favourable moment be enforced. Accordingly, while he accepted the patriciate from Zeno, and so legitimised his position as an imperial minister in the eyes of Italy, he fortified himself by assuming another title which must have expressed his relation to the barbarian army, viz. the title of king, *rex*. We do not know what solemnity or form accompanied the assumption of this title. But its effect was to give Odovacar the double character of a German king as well as an imperial officer. . . . So Odovacar was king of the Germans who through him obtained settlements in Italy, while he was also a Patricius, acting under the authority of the Emperor Zeno. There was thus theoretically no detachment of Italy from the Empire in the days of Odovacar. . . . The position of Odovacar was still further regularised a few years later (480) by the death of Julius Nepos.

The death of Julius Nepos is an event which has some significance; it marks the cessation of a separate line of emperors in the west. But if I have made clear the circumstances of the revolution headed by Odovacar, you will perceive that this event, though of importance in the history of Italy, has not the importance and significance which has been commonly ascribed to it. The year 476 has been generally taken as a great landmark, and the event has been commonly described as the fall of the Western Empire. This unfortunate expression conveys a wholly erroneous idea of the bearings of Odovacar's revolution. . . . This event concerns specially the history of Italy, in the same way as the settlements of the Visigoths and Burgundians concerned the history of Gaul; and the settlement of the Germans in Italy does not directly affect the western provinces as a whole. It is then a misleading misuse of words to speak of a fall of the Western Empire in 476: the revolution of that year marks but a stage, and that not the last stage, in the encroachments of the barbarian settlers in the western provinces.

Rome's Eastern Sector Survives as the Byzantine Empire

Mark Nadis

Although the western Roman throne became vacant in 476, the eastern one, situated at the royal court in Constantinople, remained occupied for many centuries to come. A number of modern historians point to this fact when they emphasize the survival of Roman civilization rather than its fall. Here, Mark Nadis, a former professor at Los Angeles Valley College, provides a summary of how the eastern Roman realm, which steadily mutated into the Byzantine Empire, maintained and drew on the laws, architecture, and other aspects of Roman civilization.

Gibbon's famous *Decline and Fall of the Roman Empire* does not end with the Western Empire. The Eastern Roman Empire endured for more than a thousand years with only a brief interruption in the thirteenth century, but it was not simply a continuation of Western culture. The Eastern or Byzantine Empire had a flavor and tradition of its own, distinct from Rome. Not only did it make original contributions in art, architecture, and theology, but it preserved a good deal of ancient Greek thought, which later became incorporated into Western philosophy. Byzantium also Christianized the Slavs, and this process involved the creation of a Russian alphabet. (Some Slavic peoples moved west and were absorbed by Western Christianity, but the vast bulk ultimately settled in the Balkan Peninsula and fell under the influence of Constantinople or remained on the eastern steppes.) Some of the difference between East and West was a result of the schism which developed between the Roman and the Orthodox (Byzantine) Church; part was because Greek rather than Latin was the language of the upper class in the East.

The Reign of Justinian (527–565)

Justinian's reign may be looked on as the last effort to reestablish the old Roman Empire, yet his expansionist policy in North Africa, Italy, and Spain hardly survived his death. Africa was held until Roman rule collapsed there in the next century under Muslim assault. Taxes were increased to the point where distress became widespread despite commercial prosperity. If Justinian had been less obsessed with his imperial dream, he would have realized that the Danube frontier was more vital to his interest than anything the West could offer. Indeed, had his successors attempted to defend his conquests, the Eastern Empire would have been destroyed in the seventh century. The best one can say is that he brought the West in contact with Roman civilization.

Justinian's greatest achievement was the codification of the Roman law, a great feat he shared with his eminent jurist, Tribonian. Their first task was to assemble the *Codex*, the laws of the Roman Empire. Next the Tribonian committee edited the laws and decisions of the Roman Republic. This collection, called the *Digest*, was an even greater achievement. The commission's work was completed with the *Institutes*, a text book of principles for law students, and the *Novellae*, a collection of the laws of Justinian himself. All were in Latin except the latter, which was written in Greek for the benefit of the predominantly Greek-speaking empire. Perhaps no work except the Bible has had a more profound effect on Western Civilization. It was from the *Codex* that Europe rediscovered Roman law in the twelfth century.

Justinian also initiated other administrative reforms. He pruned the official bureaucracy to render it more efficient, fixed salaries for all officials, and began a more regular method of recruiting them. He established state industrial monopolies, including silk manufacture (silk worm eggs had been smuggled out of China in hollow canes). He issued new and effective regulations governing traders in the great cities; and as were earlier Roman emperors, Justinian was a great builder of roads, fortifications, and aqueducts. The most splendid of his many churches was the Cathedral of the Holy Wisdom (Hagia Sophia) at Constantinople.

The Byzantine Economy

There have been few states whose economic life was as closely regulated as that of the Eastern Roman Empire. The manufacturer who wanted to lay in a stock of raw materials had to contact a specific supplier. Certain items such as yellow soap, known as "Gaul Soap," did not enter the market but were reserved exclusively for the emperor's use. There was an attempt to maintain complete secrecy of manufacturing processes; producers dealt directly with one another, consumers directly with producers, and middlemen were eliminated.

But Byzantium's prosperity was not due to regulation alone; it resulted as much, if not more, from her geographical location, her financial system, and the skill of her people. The city lay astride the main trade route between East and West. Riches from every corner of the earth found their way into Byzantine warehouses. From India came spices and gem stones; from Persia came beautiful carpets; from North Russia came wheat, salt fish, caviar, slaves, and furs. The Byzantines did not bother to seek commercial outlets—trade came to them—but in time this policy proved to be a mistake as more active people seized and exploited commercial traffic through the straits and in the eastern Mediterranean.

The Eastern Church and State

Byzantine religion was more mystical, less legalistic and rational than that of the West. It employed gorgeous ceremonies and rituals, magnificent church interiors, and the lavish use of incense.

The chief official of the Church of Constantinople was the patriarch. He was nominated by the emperor and was subject to dismissal at any time. He was, however, the head of the Slavic Church, and the Slavs were rarely within the political boundaries of the empire. An ousted patriarch could cause trouble because the clergy and the monks would strongly support him. On several occasions a patriarch commanded more power than the emperor himself. An independent tribal chief would tend to think twice before accepting Eastern Christianity, yet if the emperor were his political enemy, he might bring some influence to bear through the patriarch. On the other hand, if he submitted to Rome instead of Constantinople, the Roman Church insisted on the use of Latin, a language incomprehensible to most Slavs. The Eastern Church, on the other hand, encouraged the use of the Slavic vernaculars.

The patriarch of Constantinople was theoretically subject to the spiritual leadership of the pope, but the pope was theoretically subject to the Eastern emperor as the true heir of Constantine. This arrangement was probably convenient for the pope, who could call upon the Eastern emperor for mil-

The Byzantine Legacy

In this excerpt from his history of the Byzantine Empire, scholar John J. Norwich points out that the Byzantines, who ensured the survival of many Roman ideas and institutions, left behind a rich cultural legacy of their own.

The Roman Empire of the East was founded by Constantine the Great on Monday, 11 May 330; it came to an end on Tuesday, 29 May 1453. During those one thousand, one hundred and twenty-three years and eighteen days, eighty-eight men and women occupied the imperial throne. . . . Of those eighty-eight, a few—Constantine himself, Justinian, Heraclius, the two Basils, Alexius Comnenus—possessed true greatness; a few—Phocas, Michael III, Zoe and the Angeli—were contemptible; the vast majority were brave, upright, God-fearing men who did their best, with greater or lesser degrees of success. Byzantium may not have lived up to its highest ideals, but it certainly did not deserve the reputation which . . . it acquired in the eighteenth and nineteenth centuries [namely that of a corrupt, only marginally important realm]. The Byzantines were, on the contrary, a deeply religious society in which illiteracy—at least among the middle and upper classes—was virtually unknown, and in which one Emperor after another was renowned for his scholarship; a society which alone

itary aid, while the emperor after the time of Justinian was not interested in exercising any rights over the pope. The final split between Constantinople and Rome in 1054 was supposedly over a theological question, but in actual fact, the patriarch was in authority in the East because he was supported by a fanatically anti-Western people and clergy. Even under Muslim assault in the fifteenth century, the Eastern clergy would not consider union with the papacy as the price of military help from the West.

The Reign of Leo III (717–740)

The work of Leo III has sometimes been regarded as a second foundation of empire. Justinian's policy of expansion had been abandoned once and for all, and much of what had

---

preserved much of the heritage of Greek and Latin antiquity, during these dark centuries in the West when the lights of learning were almost extinguished; a society, finally, which produced the astonishing phenomenon of Byzantine art. . . .

One of the first and most brilliant of twentieth-century Philhellenes [lovers of Greek culture], Robert Byron, maintained that the greatness of Byzantium lay in what he described as "the Triple Fusion": that of a Roman body, a Greek mind and an oriental, mystical soul. Certainly these three strands were always present, and were largely responsible for the Empire's unique character: at bottom, however, the Byzantines were human like the rest of us, victims of the same weaknesses and subject to the same temptations, deserving of praise and of blame much as we are ourselves. What they do not deserve is the obscurity to which for centuries we have condemned them. Their follies were many, as were their sins; but much should surely be forgiven for the beauty they left behind them and the heroism with which they and their last brave Emperor met their end, in one of those glorious epics of world history that has passed into legend and is remembered with equal pride by victors and vanquished alike.

John J. Norwich, *A Short History of Byzantium*. New York: Knopf, 1997, pp. 382–84.

formerly been under Byzantine rule was lost to the Muslims forever. But the lands that remained were compact and manageable and a good economic base. Between them, Leo and his son ruled for fifty years, and under them Constantinople recovered her former prosperity. The tax system was reformed, and the army was made a permanent professional force. A new revised code, more humane and Christian than that of Justinian, was provided.

The first prohibition of the use of images in the Church was made by Leo III in 725. Prior to this time images and icons (holy pictures) had been very popular in Constantinople, but Leo claimed the practice was equivalent to idol worship. (The Church's admission of images in worship in the third and fourth centuries had been significant, for it preserved the Graeco-Roman artistic traditions.) Leo was a Syrian by origin, and it is probable that the practice of the Muslims and the Jews who eschewed religious images had influenced him. Leo's soldiers were instructed to break up images, and Leo's son Constantine vigorously carried out an iconoclastic policy to the bitter disappointment of the monks who made their living making images. So severe was the conflict that the empire and the papacy severed relations during the controversy.

The final restoration of the icons came in 843 when the regent Theodora of Constantinople called another council which approved the use of images. The monks had triumphed (and the Hellenic [Greek] spirit had triumphed over the Judaic concept), but even so there were no more sculptured images in the Byzantine Church. Flat images took their place.

Architecture and Art

In the late imperial period realistic portraiture was still seen in statuary and coins. The art of mosaics—composing a pictorial composition from very small colored stones—became refined. Mosaics, too, tended to reflect daily life. In graphic representation the old Graeco-Roman convention was lost; figures became flat, the background had no depth, and draperies seemed to be empty of bodies. This new style appeared in illustrated Gospel books of Asia Minor in the sixth century and at the same time in the decoration of churches in Syria and Asia Minor.

The Roman Basilica—characterized by a broad nave and side aisles—became the model for churches. A transept at right angles was frequently added to the long main section, giving the whole the configuration of a cross. The most famous monument to Byzantine architecture is the great Church of the Holy Wisdom (Hagia Sophia) opened by Justinian in 537. Used as a mosque today, it is preserved in fairly good condition, with minarets added at the four corners. Within, there are narrow circular steps behind the columns leading to galleries near the top of the enormous Oriental dome. The huge stones which make up the floor of the galleries are irregular and have large cracks between them. From the gallery the view of the interior is most impressive. The columns of the interior, derived from the Greek, are so modified that a new order has resulted. Roman, Oriental, and Greek elements of Byzantine civilization are beautifully synthesized in this church.

Survival of Roman Culture in the West

Charles Freeman

While the Byzantine court maintained a remnant of the old Roman administrative apparatus in the East, many aspects of Roman civilization survived in the small "successor states" that grew up amidst the wreckage of the western Empire. Scholar Charles Freeman, who has written extensively about the ancient Romans, here examines the transition to the Middle Ages in the West. His informative discussion includes not only the Ostrogothic, Frankish, and other early successor states and the role played by Christianity, but also the contributions of a handful of dedicated scholars who had the foresight to copy some of the old Greek and Roman literary texts and thereby preserve them for future generations.

With the collapse of the old administration local populations were now coming to terms with their new Germanic rulers. The degree of change involved may not have been enormous especially as in many areas accommodation had been taking place over decades and without major disruption. There is increasing archaeological evidence that long-range trading routes remained intact, certainly between cities, until the early sixth century. At the Schola Praeconum in Rome a refuse dump dating from about 430–40 contained *amphorae* with oil from Tunisia, wine from the eastern Mediterranean, and lamps and red-slip table ware from north Africa. The trade does not appear to have been disrupted by the Vandal invasion of Africa. Naples was also importing olive oil from north Africa as well as perfumes from

Excerpted from *Egypt, Greece, and Rome: Civilizations of the Ancient Mediterranean*, by Charles Freeman. Copyright ©1996 by Charles Freeman. Reprinted with permission from Oxford University Press.

Asia Minor, though trade with north Africa appears to have declined after 500. In the countryside, however, there is less evidence of imported goods and rural areas may have found themselves isolated. The villa economy around Monte Cassino in Italy seems to have collapsed as early as A.D. 400.

Romans and Germans Learn to Live Together

The collapse of the administrative structure did not mean that Roman culture vanished. In most areas 'Romans' continued to form the vast majority of the population and many of the incoming German peoples were already Romanized through service in the Roman army or through trading contacts. . . . Germans were thrown into close contact with those local taxpayers whose tax was assigned to them. It was in their interest to maintain the systems of landownership which provided the tax. Throughout the former empire there are, in fact, very few cases of barbarians actually dispossessing 'Roman' landowners. (The confiscation of estates by the Vandals around Carthage is an exception.) In short, accommodation between Romans and newcomers rather than confrontation seems to have been the norm.

The letters of the Gallic aristocrat Sidonius Apollinaris provide a fine picture of how a sophisticated man, schooled in classical traditions, could survive. Sidonius . . . had inherited a beautiful if remote estate in the Auvergne [in Gaul]. Here he cultivated the life of a landowner and, like many of his class, became a bishop, of Clermont in 470. In 475 when his city was besieged by Visigoths he directed its defence, but after its defeat he worked hard to cultivate relationships with his new overlords. He recognized that the Visigoths offered the best hope of defence against other attacks and to sustain the relationship he was even prepared to visit the Visigothic king Theodoric to play backgammon with him. The appearance and manners of those Germans billeted on his estate he found less palatable.

Sidonius' experiences provide a reminder that the church survived with its administrative structure intact. Its estates were large and could support its clergy. As the clergy were exempt from taxation and military service there was no shortage of recruits. In fact the church took an important role as protector of the poor. In Gaul and Italy a quarter of the church's revenue was earmarked for widows and the poor. The fifth and sixth centuries saw the emergence of a range of charitable institutions, hospitals, hospices for reception of pilgrims, and orphanages, and this role of the church was to be sustained in the centuries that followed.

While the church survived as a force for cohesion, so then did Roman law. . . . One of the last joint achievements of the eastern and western empires had been, in fact, the Law Code issued by Theodosius II (emperor in the east 408–50). It was a definitive collection of imperial laws issued from the time of Constantine onwards, proclaimed throughout the empire in 438. Many German rulers now adopted it for their 'Roman' subjects. King Alaric II made an abridgement of the Code for his Aquitanian subjects in 506 while the Ostrogoth king Theodoric promulgated it in Italy about 500. The use of Roman law perpetuated the concept that the state should take responsibility for justice on behalf of an individual and that there were personal rights which should be protected. However, it also meant that other features of Roman society such as slavery persisted with legal support. (The trade in slaves in England was forbidden for the first time only in 1102.)

The administrative functions of the church may have helped to sustain urban life but most towns in the west were mere shells of what they had been. In the north-west of the empire towns had virtually ceased to exist after A.D. 400. Others were reduced to little more than markets for peasant exchanges, temporary barracks for soldiers on campaign, and fortified refuges to be used in times of trouble. Lyons [in Gaul] had covered 160 hectares in its heyday—by the sixth century it was down to twenty. Cathedrals might still be built in cities but in Gaul the Franks tended to build their churches on the sites of Roman estates with villages growing up later around them. Communities now centred on the courts of the Germanic kings or monasteries. This was now a rural world and its horizons were inevitably narrower than they had been.

Theodoric and the Ostrogoths in Italy

The best-documented example of how Roman and German lived alongside each other is the kingdom of the Ostrogoth Theodoric in Italy (493–526). The Ostrogoths were made up of those Goths who had remained north of the borders of the empire under the domination of the Huns (in contrast to the forerunners of the Visigoths who had fled over the border in the 370s). After the collapse of Attila's empire in the 450s, they had moved into the empire. There was a power struggle for leadership which led eventually in 484 to the emergence of a new leader, Theodoric. Theodoric had spent ten years of his early life as a hostage in Constantinople (461–71) and so had absorbed some elements of classical culture. However, when back with his own people, he showed no inhibitions in attacking the eastern empire. It seems that the eastern emperor Zeno decided, in 488, to divert him by sending him to Italy to overthrow Odoacer. After enduring a long siege in Ravenna Odoacer surrendered but was murdered by Theodoric. Theodoric was now the most powerful man in Italy.

It has been estimated that Theodoric may have had a following of some 100,000 Ostrogoths. Archaeological and literary evidence combine to suggest they were settled mostly in the north-east of Italy, probably to protect Theodoric's new kingdom against invasion from the north by other German tribes. Theodoric consolidated his position steadily. He guarded against counter-attack from the east by assuming control over Pannonia in 505. When the Visigothic kingdom collapsed in Provence [in Gaul] in 508, Theodoric annexed the province and also annexed Visigothic Spain in 511. Marriage links were made with the Burgundians and Vandals.

Theodoric's 'Roman' subjects numbered some four million so accommodation with them was essential. In fact, Theodoric showed much sympathy for classical civilization. After he took over Provence he wrote to its 'Roman' inhabitants, 'Having been recalled to your old freedom by the gift of God, clothe yourselves with manners befitting the toga, eschew [avoid] barbarism and put aside the cruelty of your minds, because it is not fitting for you to live according to strange customs in the time of our just rule'. . . . The Romans were encouraged to use their own laws for disputes among themselves. It helped that Theodoric took a personal interest in Rome, even restoring some of the buildings there and allowing the senators to retain their status and prestige. Although Rome, like other cities in the west, was in decline with a population now of probably only 100,000, there was a revival of the city's ancient pride. The corn handouts were resumed and games were held when Theodoric visited the city in 500. Images of the emperor were replaced by pictures of Romulus and Remus suckled by the wolf. . . .

In short, Theodoric quickly gained the respect of Romans (even being compared by some to the emperors Trajan and Valentinian). A number, including the scholar Cassiodorus (whose letters provide one of the best sources of the reign), the senator Symmachus (descendant of the pagan Symmachus of the fourth century), and Symmachus' son-in-law, the senator and philosopher Boethius, served the regime as senior civil servants. . . . Theodoric tolerated orthodox Christianity, and in Ravenna, which Theodoric made his capital. . . . In some cases the barriers between Roman and Goth were broken down. Many of the wealthier Goths appear to have been attracted by the Roman way of life. Some took Roman names, converted to orthodox Christianity, and intermarried with the Roman nobility. Cassiodorus was able to write to some of his Gothic correspondents in Latin.

Boethius and Cassiodorus

In such an atmosphere classical culture could survive and even be transmitted to future generations. The major intellectual figure of Theodoric's Italy was Anicus Manlius Severinus Boethius. Boethius was from an aristocratic family which had links to at least two emperors and one bishop of Rome. He showed great intellectual promise from an early age and his life was divided between service of Theodoric and philosophical study. Among his achievements was a translation into Latin of all Aristotle's works on logic which kept Aristotle's name alive in the medieval west when all knowledge of Greek had disappeared. Boethius had hoped to go on to translating the *Dialogues* of Plato and then show

how the works of the two philosophers could be reconciled, but in 524 he was arrested on a charge of treason and bludgeoned to death after Theodoric confirmed the death sentence passed by a court in Rome. The affair is normally regarded as a black stain on Theodoric's otherwise tolerant treatment of Roman aristocrats although it is difficult to sort out who actually made the accusations against Boethius and exactly what they consisted of.

It was while awaiting his death in prison that Boethius composed the work for which he is most famous, *The Consolation of Philosophy*. It is a purely classical work which, despite being religious in tone, has not a single mention of Christ or Christianity. . . . One of the major themes explored in *The Consolation* is the apparent contradiction between the existence of an ultimate 'Good' and the everyday vagaries of fate. The individual has to lift himself above the injustices of everyday life so that he can be united with the stability of 'the Good'. . . . *The Consolation of Philosophy* became one of the most read books of medieval Europe, its comparative simplicity providing an attractive contrast to the intricate quarrels of the medieval schools of philosophy. [The thirteenth-century Italian poet] Dante claimed that it provided him with consolation after the death of his beloved Beatrice.

A century before, Augustine had argued that a training in the classics, particularly in grammar and rhetoric, was essential for any Christian. Perhaps the most distinguished of Theodoric's 'Roman' civil servants, Cassiodorus, agreed. Cassiodorus (490–c.585) argued that the best training for higher studies in Christian theology was provided by the seven liberal arts, grammar, logic, rhetoric, music, geometry, arithmetic, and astronomy. When in retirement in his fifties, he founded his own monastery at Vivarium on his family estates in southern Italy. Here he collected manuscripts both Christian and pagan and encouraged the monks to copy them, even providing a manual, *De Orthographia*, to help them resolve textual difficulties. A large number of Latin authors were preserved in this way and even some Greek texts such as Eusebius' *History of the Church* and the medical works of Galen and Hippocrates. It was partly thanks to Cassiodorus that an education in pagan classical texts was enshrined as part of the church's own education system at a time when secular schooling was in decline.

The Frankish Kingdom

While Theodoric was holding court in Italy other Germanic peoples were successfully setting up kingdoms. As early as the fourth century the Franks had been used by the Romans to keep order on the Rhine frontier, and in the disastrous years 406–7 they played some part in resisting the influx of other German invaders. Between 430 and 440 Franks are found settled between Tournai and Cambrai [in what is now France] and it was in Tournai in 1653 that the tomb of an early Frankish 'king', Childeric, was found intact. The king was surrounded by a treasury of gold and silver, two great swords with scabbards inlaid with garnets, and a rich cloak, in short all the paraphernalia of royalty. It was Childeric's son Clovis who was to expand the kingdom. He threw back the Alamanni towards the Upper Rhine and energetically disposed of rival kings. His shrewdest move was to become converted to orthodox Christianity, possibly in 498 or 499. This immediately gave him a link with the 'Roman' populations under Burgundian and Visigoth rule . . . and the support of their bishops. He now marched triumphantly into Aquitaine and, at the battle of Vouillé in 507, defeated and killed the Visigothic king, Alaric II. By the time of his death, probably in 511, Clovis had laid the foundations of a large Frankish kingdom underpinned by orthodox Christianity.

The events of the next two centuries are confused. After Clovis' death his kingdom was split between four of his sons although these seem to have worked together in comparative harmony. Between 533 and 548 there was once again strong centralized rule under Clovis' grandson, Theudebert I. Theudebert eliminated the Burgundian kingdom in 534 and gained Provence from the Ostrogoths in 536. He also expanded north of the Rhine and even across the Alps into Italy. For the first time in European history Franks and other Germans lived together in some form of political unity with the Rhine no longer a barrier between them. Theudebert deliberately cultivated an imperial presence in the old Roman style. He presided over games in the hippodrome at Arles and for his coinage adopted the eastern *solidus* (first minted by Constantine) with his name and title substituted for that of the eastern emperor. The kingdom disintegrated after Theudebert's death but was reunited again by a great-grandson of Clovis, Chlothar I, in 558. Under Chlothar II (584–629) and Dagobert (629–38) the Frankish kingdom was to survive as the most effective kingdom of the west.

Changes in Spain and Italy

The Visigothic kingdom in Spain had to endure annexation by the Ostrogoths and invasion by the Byzantines . . . before it re-emerged as a strong and centralized kingdom at the end of the sixth century. Leovigild (569–86) achieved the reunification of most of the peninsula through military means, finally defeating the Suevic kingdom in 585. . . .

In the seventh century the Visigothic kingdom was to compete with the Frankish as the most stable and intellectually fertile in Europe. The most influential of its scholars was Isidore, bishop of Seville from about 600 to 636. Isidore's main contribution to political life was the development of a theory of Christian kingship in which the ruler must shine through the exercise of his faith. However, his contribution to scholarship was as great. In his twenty-volume *Etymologies*, Isidore collected a vast range of earlier material to serve as a foundation for the understanding of the meanings of Latin words. He was a determined advocate of a traditional classical education for the clergy, insisting that it was better for Christians that they read the pagan authors than remain ignorant of them. Like Cassiodorus in Italy, he set in hand the copying of manuscripts, and classical learning was preserved as a feature of education more successfully in Spain than in any other western state. . . .

The attempt [by leaders in Constantinople] to reconquer Italy was not a success. . . . Justinian had hoped to restore some form of classical, albeit Christian, civilization to the west but wars often achieve the opposite of their hopes. One result of the eastern intervention in Italy was the disappearance of the senatorial aristocracy. Many were simply eliminated by the Goths as suspected traitors. In 547 the Gothic king, Totila, had taken Rome, now reduced to a population of some 30,000, and seized the treasures of the senatorial palaces. Many senators had simply fled with all they could carry. The last of the Gothic leaders, Teias, massacred some three hundred children of senatorial families whom he was holding as hostages. The villa economy, on which the senators' wealth depended, also seems to have disappeared at the same time, doubtless dislocated by the protracted wars. The senate ceased to meet in the 580s and it is in these years that the image of Rome as an abandoned city, its great monuments falling into ruin, first emerges.

There is, however, one magnificent set of survivals from these troubled years, the churches of Ravenna. The city had been the emperor's capital from 402 but achieved its full glory under Theodoric, one which was sustained when Ravenna came under eastern control after 540. The splendour of these churches lies in their mosaics. Mosaics had originally been used only on floors, but from the fifth century they were increasingly used for walls and vaults. . . .

When Justinian had finally achieved some sort of victory in Italy in 554 he attempted to reimpose an imperial system of administration, staffed by eastern officials. It was bitterly resented by the demoralized population. In any case, there was little in the way of an administrative structure left outside that provided by the church. . . .

The Church and Latin Language

Up to the fifth century the bishops of Rome, though maintaining some authority in the church as a whole as the proclaimed successors of Peter, had played little part in formulating Christian doctrine. The Christian world was predominantly Greek, the great councils of the church at which doctrine had been decided took place either at Constantinople (381, 553) or even further east (Nicaea (325), Ephesus (431), Chalcedon (451)). (At the Council of Constantinople in 381 an attempt by western bishops to move things their way was met with cries of 'Christ came in the

East!'.) The dominant figures in these councils had been the emperors not individual bishops.

Rome's attempts to exert influence were not helped by the comparative isolation of the city from the east and the persistence in Rome of a strong pagan élite. There were individual Italian bishops, Ambrose in Milan, for instance, who found themselves in a position to exercise greater power than a bishop based in Rome. It was not until the Council of Chalcedon in 451, when the so-called *tome* (letter) of Leo was read (in his absence), that 'for the first time Rome took a determining role in the definition of Christian dogma' . . . and even here there was a challenge to Rome's claims to primacy when, to Leo's fury, Constantinople's status was raised to be second only to that of Rome (a move designed as much to raise its authority above the older Christian bishoprics of Antioch and Alexandria as to challenge Rome). The Council held in Constantinople under Justinian's auspices in 553 conducted its business totally independently of Rome.

When in 590 a new bishop of Rome, Gregory (540–604), was consecrated, it seemed that the supremacy of the Greek east in defining Christianity would continue. Gregory had spent several years in Constantinople and had expressed some sympathy for the eastern position on doctrine. The emperors must have hoped that he could be controlled. These hopes were soon dashed. Gregory was a Roman aristocrat (in fact a former City Prefect) and his affection and concern for the city remained strong. He fed its often starving population from his own estates. Despite his stay in Constantinople he was not learned in Greek and represented the new clerical culture of the west, in which learning in the Latin classics was combined with a devout and somewhat austere Christianity, but remained always subservient to it. His happiest days, he recalled, were those when he was living as a monk in a community he had founded in Rome.

Gregory doggedly set out on a new path. The bishop of Rome was to be the presiding force in Christian Europe with his fellow but subordinate bishops strengthened as leaders of the Christian communities. It was a sophisticated vision which owed much to the theology of Augustine but rested ultimately on the direct succession Gregory claimed from the apostle Peter. The foundations had been laid of the medieval papacy. They were reinforced by the widening doctrinal split with the east, and a growing isolation from the traditional Greek-speaking centres of Christianity as the leading members of the western church (Augustine is one example) were unable any longer to understand Greek. . . .

Yet few in the late sixth century could have predicted the later supremacy over Europe of the popes. Rome as a city was by now isolated, little more than a few churches encircling the ruined centre. The Lombards had overrun many of the larger Italian cities and Gregory had only the most fragile of contacts with the rest of Europe. The mission he sent to England which successfully converted the Anglo-Saxons was in the circumstances a magnificent achievement. The acceptance of papal authority was slow (the Irish St Columban was still arguing in the seventh century that if any one bishop had the right to exert supreme authority in the church that was surely the bishop of Jerusalem), but there is no doubt that Gregory's reign marks a turning point in the history of Christianity. . . .

Not least of the achievements of Gregory and his fellow bishops was to ensure the survival of classical Latin as the language of church law and administration in the Middle Ages and beyond. There was also a more colloquial Latin, the language of ordinary people of the empire. (In 813 a council of bishops at Tours ruled that sermons had to be in *rustica Romana lingua*, colloquial Latin while, presumably, the rest of the service continued in classical Latin.) The relationship of the two has been much discussed but . . . there were significant differences even in the early empire. It was from the local dialects of Latin that the Romance languages appear to have emerged in those areas where the Roman population was a majority, the Iberian peninsula, Italy, France, and Romania. A barrier between these areas and those further north where German became the majority language has lasted from the sixth century to the present day and is a fine reminder that despite the collapse of the Empire its legacy in Europe persisted.

Chapter 3

Factors Contributing to Rome's Fall

Turning|Points

IN WORLD HISTORY

Gibbon Opens the Debate on Rome's Fall

Edward Gibbon

The major early milestone in modern studies and debates about the fall of Rome was English historian Edward Gibbon's masterpiece, *The Decline and Fall of the Roman Empire*, published in the late 1700s. A relatively short but decidedly crucial section titled "General Observations of the Fall of the Roman Empire in the West" is excerpted here. Among the causes he names for the Empire's decline and fall are its "immoderate greatness," or its having become too large and complex to govern itself efficiently and safely; the self-indulgence of the upper-classes; the division of the Empire, which, he says, weakened it; the barbarian invasions; and the negative effects of the Christian church and its pacifistic teachings, which supposedly weakened Rome's traditional military spirit. Considering these and other problems the Empire encountered, Gibbon concludes, it is surprising that it managed to last as long as it did.

The Greeks, after their country had been reduced into a province, imputed the triumphs of Rome, not to the merit, but to the FORTUNE, of the republic. The inconstant goddess, who so blindly distributes and resumes her favours, had *now* consented (such was the language of envious flattery) to resign her wings, to descend from her globe, and to fix her firm and immutable throne on the banks of the Tyber [the Tiber River, which flows near Rome; i.e., the gods have now come to favor Rome over Greece]. A wiser Greek [Polybius, who wrote a history of Rome in the second century B.C.], who has

Excerpted from "General Observations on the Fall of the Roman Empire in the West," by Edward Gibbon in *The Decline and Fall of the Roman Empire*, edited by David Womersley. Copyright ©1994 by David Womersley. Reprinted with permission from Chatto & Windus, a division of Random House, UK.

composed, with a philosophic spirit, the memorable history of his own times, deprived his countrymen of this vain and delusive comfort, by opening to their view the deep foundations of the greatness of Rome. The fidelity of the citizens to each other, and to the state, was confirmed by the habits of education, and the prejudices of religion. Honour, as well as virtue, was the principle of the republic; the ambitious citizens laboured to deserve the solemn glories of a triumph; and the ardour of the Roman youth was kindled into active emulation, as often as they beheld the domestic images of their ancestors. The temperate struggles of the patricians and plebeians had finally established the firm and equal balance of the constitution, which united the freedom of popular assemblies, with the authority and wisdom of a senate, and the executive powers of a regal magistrate. When the consul displayed the standard of the republic, each citizen bound himself, by the obligation of an oath, to draw his sword in the cause of his country, till he had discharged the sacred duty by a military service of ten years. This wise institution continually poured into the field the rising generations of freemen and soldiers; and their numbers were reinforced by the warlike and populous states of Italy, who, after a brave resistance, had yielded to the valour, and embraced the alliance, of the Romans. The sage historian [again Polybius], who excited the virtue of the younger Scipio, and beheld the ruin of Carthage, has accurately described their military system; their levies, arms, exercises, subordination, marches, encampments; and the invincible legion, superior in active strength to the Macedonian phalanx of Philip and Alexander. From these institutions of peace and war, Polybius has deduced the spirit and success of a people, incapable of fear, and impatient of repose. The ambitious design of conquest, which might have been defeated by the seasonable conspiracy of mankind, was attempted and achieved; and the perpetual violation of justice was maintained by the political virtues of prudence and courage. The arms of the republic, sometimes vanquished in battle, always victorious in war, advanced with rapid steps to the Euphrates, the Danube, the Rhine, and the Ocean; and the images of gold, or silver, or brass, that might serve to represent the nations and their kings, were successively broken by the *iron* monarchy of Rome.

Division and Decay

The rise of a city, which swelled into an empire, may deserve, as a singular prodigy, the reflection of a philosophic mind. But the decline of Rome was the natural and inevitable effect of immoderate greatness. Prosperity ripened the principle of decay; the causes of destruction multiplied with the extent of conquest; and as soon as time or accident had removed the artificial supports, the stupendous fabric yielded to the pressure of its own weight. The story of its ruin is simple and obvious; and instead of inquiring *why* the Roman empire was destroyed, we should rather be surprised that it had subsisted so long. The victorious legions, who, in distant wars acquired the vices of strangers and mercenaries, first oppressed the freedom of the republic, and afterwards violated the majesty of the Purple [i.e., the authority of the emperors]. The emperors, anxious for their personal safety and the public peace, were reduced to the base expedient of corrupting the discipline which rendered them alike formidable to their sovereign and to the enemy; the vigour of the military government was relaxed, and finally dissolved, by the partial institutions of Constantine; and the Roman world was overwhelmed by a deluge of Barbarians.

The decay of Rome has been frequently ascribed to the translation of the seat of empire; but this history has already shewn, that the powers of government were *divided*, rather than *removed*. The throne of Constantinople was erected in the East; while the West was still possessed by a series of emperors who held their residence in Italy, and claimed their equal inheritance of the legions and provinces. This dangerous novelty impaired the strength, and fomented the vices, of a double reign: the instruments of an oppressive and arbitrary system were multiplied; and a vain emulation of luxury, not of merit, was introduced and supported between the degenerate successors of Theodosius. Extreme distress, which unites the virtue of a free people, embitters the factions, of declining monarchy. The hostile favourites of Arcadius and

Honorius betrayed the republic to its common enemies; and the Byzantine court beheld with indifference, perhaps with pleasure, the disgrace of Rome, the misfortunes of Italy, and the loss of the West. Under the succeeding reigns, the alliance of the two empires was restored; but the aid of the Oriental Romans was tardy, doubtful, and ineffectual; and the national schism of the Greeks and Latins was enlarged by the perpetual difference of language and manners, of interest, and even of religion. Yet the salutary event approved in some measure the judgment of Constantine. During a long period of decay, his impregnable city repelled the victorious armies of Barbarians, protected the wealth of Asia, and commanded, both in peace and war, the important streights which connect the Euxine [Black] and Mediterranean seas. The foundation of Constantinople more essentially contributed to the preservation of the East, than to the ruin of the West.

Negative Effects of the Church

As the happiness of a *future* life is the great object of religion, we may hear without surprise or scandal, that the introduction, or at least the abuse, of Christianity, had some influence on the decline and fall of the Roman empire. The clergy successfully preached the doctrines of patience and pusillanimity [cowardice]; the active virtues of society were discouraged; and the last remains of military spirit were buried in the cloyster: a large portion of public and private wealth was consecrated to the specious demands of charity and devotion; and the soldiers pay was lavished on the useless multitudes of both sexes, who could only plead the merits of abstinence and chastity. Faith, zeal, curiosity, and the more earthly passions of malice and ambition, kindled the flame of theological discord; the church, and even the state, were distracted by religious factions, whose conflicts were sometimes bloody, and always implacable; the attention of the emperors was diverted from [military] camps to synods [church meetings]; the Roman world was oppressed by a new species of tyranny; and the persecuted sects became the secret enemies of their country. Yet party-spirit, however pernicious or absurd, is a principle of union as well as of dissention. The bishops, from eighteen hundred pulpits, inculcated [taught] the duty of passive obedience to a lawful and Orthodox sovereign; their frequent assemblies, and perpetual correspondence, maintained the communion of distant churches; and the benevolent temper of the gospel was strengthened, though confined, by the spiritual alliance of the Catholics. The sacred indolence of the monks was devoutly embraced by a servile and effeminate [unmanly] age; but if superstition had not afforded a decent retreat, the same vices would have tempted the unworthy Romans to desert, from baser motives, the standard of the republic. Religious precepts are easily obeyed, which indulge and sanctify the natural inclinations of their votaries; but the pure and genuine influence of Christianity may be traced in its beneficial, though imperfect, effects on the Barbarian proselytes of the North. If the decline of the Roman empire was hastened by the conversion of Constantine, his victorious religion broke the violence of the fall, and mollified the ferocious temper of the conquerors.

The Western Empire's Economy Deteriorated

F.W. Walbank

This appraisal of the decline of the economy of the later Empire is from *The Awful Revolution*, by F.W. Walbank, a distinguished scholar formerly of the University of Liverpool in England. Walbank drew the book's title from a famous line from Edward Gibbon's *The Decline and Fall of the Roman Empire:* "This awful revolution [i.e., Rome's fall] may be usefully applied to the instruction of the present age." The deterioration of the western Roman economy, says Walbank, was due to several factors. These included: a debasing and devaluation of the coinage, contributing to inflation (a rise in prices accompanied by a decrease in the purchasing power of money); a decline in the volume of trade; the heavy burden of taxation; and a substantial increase in the rift between rich and poor, accompanied by the development of widespread serfdom.

One expression of the general crisis of the economic structure was the deterioration of the currency. After the drop in the silver content of the *denarius* to 50 per cent under Septimus Severus (A.D. 193–211) until the reign of Gallienus (A.D. 253–68) the metal ratio between silver and gold, and the purchasing power of the coinage, seem to have remained steady, though gradually more alloy was introduced into the silver. But after A.D. 256 the quality of the silver coins deteriorated so rapidly that they were very soon no more than silver-washed bronze. Diocletian attempted to re-establish the currency with new silver and gold pieces; the *aureus* weighing 1/60 of a pound was equivalent to 24 *argentei*, each 1/96

Excerpted from F.W. Walbank, *The Awful Revolution: The Decline of the Roman Empire in the West* (Toronto: University of Toronto Press, 1969). Copyright ©1969 by F.W. Walbank.

of a pound. Meanwhile silver-washed bronze continued to circulate, and in the *Edict on Prices*, published in A.D. 301, a pound of gold is valued at 50,000 *denarii*, which gives an *aureus*: *denarius* ratio of 1:833.3.

Constantine struck a new gold coin, the *solidus*, weighing ½₂ of a pound, and maintained Diocletian's *argenteus*. This system, with minor modifications, which were perhaps intended to compensate for changes in the relative values of the two metals, was maintained throughout the fourth century and beyond; indeed the *solidus* continued to be minted virtually without change until A.D. 1070, when debased specimens began to appear. . . .

Meanwhile, however, bronze or silvered bronze continued to decline in value, perhaps because the government, concerned only with its own fiscal advantage, went on issuing more and more while insisting on having its taxes paid only in gold. . . . The ratio between the *denarius*, now merely a notional sum, a fraction of the smallest bronze coin, and the *solidus* was constantly changing to the detriment of the former. Evidence from Egyptian papyri shows that in A.D. 324 the *solidus* was worth 4,350 *denarii* in Egypt; it rapidly fell to 54,000, to 150,000, to 180,000 and by about A.D. 338 was equivalent to 257,000. Just over ten years later it was worth 5,760,000 *denarii* and by the later years of the century 45,000,000. . . .

At first sight such an inflation might be expected to have put an end to all normal economic life based on a money economy. But this was not so. Naturally commodities tended to rise in price in terms of the currency that was being debased; for example, we find the price of a loaf of bread at Ephesus doubling between the reign of Trajan and the decade A.D. 220–30. Moreover in any inflation wages tend to lag behind prices, and this would of course add to the economic distress. On the other hand, a modern inflation in which notes are multiplied results in a fall in the value of all notes, new and old: but the debasing of silver only affects the new coins, which therefore tend to be re-tariffed [revalued], leaving the older specimens untouched. In fact, inscriptions make a sharp distinction between 'old coins' and 'new'. Hoarded money—and hoarding was among the commonest forms of saving in ancient times—maintained its value; and the main loss was sustained by people who had lent large sums with an agreement for fixed repayments, and by those who had the misfortune to accept the new coins before the new rate was established. Inflation introduced an element of uncertainty into business dealings, and the effects of this can be traced. But after each fall in the silver content of the *denarius* there was a period of stability, during which commerce went on as usual; and at no time did money disappear from economic life.

Taxing Both Rich and Poor

To a considerable extent, it is true, we find guild members working for a pittance or even a financial loss, and receiving recompense largely in kind; and the army and state employees generally were on a similar footing. But another sector of the economy, and that by no means negligible, still operated by means of money. For example, payment of taxes in kind only applied to those living on the land; for others there were taxes in gold and silver. Thus senators, in addition to the *annona* [tax in the form of foodstuffs and other supplies] levied on their estates, were liable for a special surtax, and also for the payment of a sum of gold on the occasion of the emperor's accession and each five-yearly anniversary of it; with the multiplication of emperors this could become a very considerable impost. Likewise the magistrates and council-members of the various cities were required to contribute 'crown gold', theoretically in celebration of special occasions and later, after A.D. 364, as a compulsory donation. Finally, the trading classes, including virtually anyone who pursued a gainful employment, were liable for a special tax, levied every five years on the capital involved in a business, with a minimum payment for those whose capital was negligible. This tax, which had to be paid in gold and silver, and was consequently called the *chrysargyrum*, went to pay for imperial shows and army donations; it weighed heavily on the city-dwellers, and . . . [some] parents [were] driven to enslave or prostitute their children to find the necessary sum.

With the exception of the *annona* all these taxes were paid in metal, and with the proceeds Constantine minted his gold coinage. Moreover, even the *annona* did not remain a tax exacted purely in kind. As early as A.D. 213 in Egypt, but to a much greater extent in the course of the fourth century, it had begun to evolve into yet one more tax in gold. Gradually the custom grew up of commuting the obligations of the tax into a payment in gold, a process known as *adaeratio*, and the same substitution also appears in the paying of government employees. . . . In A.D. 364 and 365 it was permitted in the payment of certain state employees, including soldiers along the Danube frontier. Twenty years later it was accepted as a general practice in Illyricum; and in the course of the fifth century it was made compulsory in the payment of officials, and appears to be recommended for the army. Finally in A.D. 439 it was adopted for troops and civil service alike, and in the west at least the period of state payments in kind was at an end. . . .

One Economy for the Rich, Another for the Poor

It is thus clear that a money economy was never completely effaced during the third and fourth centuries. For this we have the evidence of Diocletian's *Edict on Prices* and various papyri, and also the writings of the Church Fathers, who consistently assume the operation of a full money economy; we read of landowners profiting by scarcity and fearing a good harvest, sure signs of a market, of craftsmen working on their own account or as wage earners for others, and of active retail trade in everyday articles and foodstuffs, all employing money. Moreover the remarkable operation carried out by the rich and pious [Roman woman] Melania who, in the early years of the fifth century, sold all her estates scattered over the western provinces for 120,000 *solidi*, and distributed this sum in alms to the poor, would have been economically impossible under a system of barter.

In short, despite the apparent state control of all undertakings throughout the fourth and early fifth centuries, a good deal of the economic life of the provinces continued to be in the hands of small men. In so far as these small men worked for themselves or for wages, they used money. But it was, as a rule, the debased silver and bronze of the inflations, and the amount available varied from time to time and from province to province. . . . The fourth century silver hoards of Britain (which possessed no mint except during the years A.D. 296–324, when there was one at London) point to a shortage of gold; and after A.D. 400 small coins disappear completely from both Britain and the Danube area. Throughout the west the economy was much enfeebled, and in this part of the Empire, from Diocletian's time onwards, two economies seem to have existed side by side. For the general population, including the army and the state employees, there were public distributions of the necessities of life, supplemented by wages in the debased bronze currency for the purchase of small additional trifles on the free market. Simultaneously, though silver ceased to be minted by the fifth century, the rich enjoyed the advantages of a good gold coinage, with which they could buy every kind of luxury from all parts of the known world.

A Decline in Trade

These conclusions are confirmed by the picture which has survived of trade in the later Empire. . . . Fragments of Diocletian's *Edict on Prices*, which give the rates for sea transport for some fifty-seven specified trips between five named ports in the eastern half of the Empire and every part of the Mediterranean, show that sea traffic was, unlike land transport, still reasonably cheap. According to these tariffs, which are a fair reflection of conditions at the beginning of the fourth century, it was possible to ship a cargo of wheat the whole length of the Mediterranean, from Asia to Western Spain, for 26 per cent of its maximum value. Accordingly, the *Edict* presupposes a very considerable trade in objects of ordinary use of inter-provincial dimensions.

One must not, however, imagine this to have been on the same scale as the trade of the early Principate [Empire]. The evidence is sporadic and often unreliable; but what there is points to a very marked regression, especially in the western provinces. . . . During the third century this industry, like all others, suffered severely from uncertain conditions, and the invasions and social distress; but Constantine and his successors encouraged its recovery with special concessions to glass and filigree workers, provided that they undertook to pass on their skill to their children. As a result, the glass trade continued to flourish throughout the fourth century, serving the court at Trier, the nearby army, and the Gallic aristocracy. Glassware was not however used by the peasants and small artisans and traders, and though some was exported to Asia and Scandinavia, it remained a luxury and the industry never reached the scale achieved by the earlier potteries. Moreover, from the late fourth century there is a regression in quality.

This decline is part of a general trend and is to be seen in the gradual disappearance of the guilds. Under the early Empire Gallic shippers were found in every port; in the fourth century we have records of shippers from Africa, Spain and Egypt, but none from Gaul; and the new fragments of Diocletian's *Edict* suggest that the domination of the shipping trade by easterners was already beginning. The river transport guilds, which flourished earlier, have also disappeared. . . .

Further east in Germany and the Danube provinces there was a late flowering of an economy largely based on the army and the frontier trade. But it became increasingly the imperial policy to restrict the latter. First iron and bronze, then gold, were placed on the list of objects which might not be exported to the barbarians. Trade of any kind must pass through certain specified frontier posts; and very soon we find arms, wine, corn, oil, and even fish sauce included among the commodities which might not cross the border. This policy of restriction, which was largely imposed by motives of defence, killed what trade was beginning to grow up; and in A.D. 413, when the court was moved from Trier to Arles, the economy of the north suffered a fatal blow. Deserted by the rich, who fled south taking what they could, these areas deteriorated to a level not very different from that across the German frontier. . . .

Spain . . . enjoyed a modest prosperity up to the early

fourth century. There was a good deal of road construction and internal trade carried on by hawkers and pedlars; and even in the fourth century Ausonius in Gaul was receiving gifts of olive oil and the still famous fish sauce from Barcelona. . . . But the decline in the amount of evidence reflects economic decay; there is a shortage of currency—Spain had no mint—and the general picture becomes increasingly obscure. Sicily remained a land of primary production, with large estates and ranches, and some profit from the tourist traffic. For senators, who were forbidden at this time to travel elsewhere, might go to Sicily. Africa, until its seizure by the Vandals (A.D. 429–39), remained a storehouse for Rome. Carthage was still a prosperous city. But the manning of the quarries was already a serious problem by the third century, and in general the country seems never to have recovered from the pillaging which [occurred during the third-century crisis].

Italy, meanwhile, had continued to decline. In the fourth century vast tracts of land were out of cultivation, and brigandage so common that in A.D. 364 the use of horses was forbidden to shepherds and even landowners in seven provinces. By the end of the century half a million *iugera*—more than a quarter of a million acres—were lying fallow in the once smiling land of Campania; and in A.D. 450 the legal codes refer to children sold into slavery because of the starvation of their parents. For several centuries now Italy had played a passive role in imperial commerce. It no longer aimed at doing more than satisfying some of its own needs. Indeed from the time of Diocletian onwards the part of the peninsula south of the Rubicon was released from the payment of *annona*, on condition of its supplying Rome with meat, wine, wood and lime. Here as elsewhere the guilds were subordinated more and more to the needs of the State. But with the Gothic invasions of the fifth century and the cessation of corn imports from Vandal Africa, records became meagre and difficult to interpret. The evidence points to the disappearance of the guilds, and the whole organization of which they formed a part, with the collapse of the western Empire in A.D. 476.

The Rise of Large Country Estates

Until the general break-up in the fifth century, money continued to be employed throughout the western provinces; and with the adoption of *adaeratio* in all fields the fiscal experiment of collecting the taxes and paying the army and civil service to a large extent in kind came to an end. Nevertheless, particularly in the West, where towns were more recent and less frequent, this experiment had helped to consolidate a trend by no means negligible among the causes of the final disruption of the State.

As we saw, the pressure on the small man, on the guildsman and the independent peasant, the danger from the troops themselves, and the often insupportable burden of taxation and pressed labour, led more and more of the victims to take to flight; and it often happened that there was only one refuge—the large and powerful landowner. For the landlords survived and even prospered when the city men perished or, if they could escape their obligations . . ., withdrew to their estates and themselves became exclusively landlords. Moreover it is a mark of the primacy of land as the chief economic factor in the ancient world that the 'racketeers' who naturally sprang up under the bureaucracy and in the chaos of the third century . . . put their wealth, not . . . into industry, but into land. Instead of industrial monopolists they became feudal barons; and in an age in which a strongly centralized government could be influenced only by the exertion of group pressures, it is noteworthy that the great landowners constituted the most effective and powerful of such groups, more influential even than the army or the church and outstripped in this respect only by the highest members of the civil service, the lawyers and the senatorial aristocracy (who were, of course, often identical with them). By contrast the peasantry, freeholders and tenants alike, and the craftsmen, shopkeepers and merchants of the towns had no way of expressing their grievances or swaying policy in a direction favourable to their interests. Indeed, if one is to understand this age, one must draw a sharp distinction between the small man bound to his strict routine by bureaucratic codes and police sanctions and the extravagant lives of successful careerists. . . .

The manor economy which thus grew up and flourished played an important cultural part in the history of the later Empire. As the towns decayed, the manors produced for the local market; and in this way the new, mediaeval orientation of the countryside towards the manor and its owner becomes more marked, and the relationship between the latter and the surrounding district intensified. Moreover, the manors were the chief remaining market for the international luxury trade, which continued to operate even after all primary needs were being satisfied locally. The rich landowners had the means to pay for spices from the east, elaborate woods and precious stones, which not being bulky still amply repaid the risks entailed in their shipment. Such manor houses, homes of luxury and culture even in the darkest hours of the Empire, stand out as the new guardians of the ancient tradition; and to some extent they bring culture to the countryside, with which they enjoy a more intimate relationship than was ever possible for the towns, whose place they have taken. . . .

Slaves of the Land

Economically too the manorial household succeeded in bridging a gap which the classical economy had never managed to close—that between peasant proprietorship and the capitalistic plantation worked by slave labour. . . . Slavery was at this time a declining institution. Not that it disappeared entirely. . . . Indeed the rich may still have possessed slaves on what seems a tremendous scale, if we may judge from Melania, who manumitted [freed] 8,000 by a single act. Yet the slave had declined in importance; and he had been largely replaced on the land by the tenant-farmer or *colonus*. Throughout the Empire, as agriculture fell back to subsistence levels, it became convenient to parcel out large estates among poor tenants or settlers, who paid the landlord with a fixed proportion of their yield and, in certain provinces (though not in Italy), with a stipulated amount of labour annually. This labour, reminiscent of the services exacted from those holding land . . . in mediaeval times, was constantly being increased by the landlord (or, more often, by the rich

Though not traditional slaves bought from the auction block, depicted here, the coloni *were far from free.*

tenant who came between the landlord and the *colonus*) with the connivance of the imperial officials. . . .

These small tenants were originally free men, bound only by their respective contracts. But as early as Nero (A.D. 54–68) we hear of the transfer of barbarian settlers inside the Empire . . . and from the time of M. Aurelius (A.D. 161–80) it became common for the emperors to replenish the depleted fields of the provinces with German settlers defeated in war. These *tributarii*, as they were termed, though for many purposes they ranked as free men, were legally tied to their plots of land. Not unnaturally the distinction between the free Roman *colonus* and the unfree Romanized *tributarius* soon began to be blurred; and as might be expected, it was the status of the *colonus* which deteriorated. However, there were more violent forces at work than mere assimilation. As we saw, Septimius Severus (A.D. 193–211) instituted a new tax, the *annona*, which consisted of a fixed amount of produce to be provided by landowners; and this tax was further systematized at the end of the century by Diocletian, who issued a rescript laying down the quantity of foodstuffs for the production of which each estate throughout the Empire was liable, based not only on acreage, but also on the 'heads of male labour' employed, no matter what their legal status. Thus from the beginning of the third century onwards it became a matter of imperial policy to support the landlord in any measures he might take to ensure that his fields were adequately cultivated, and the fiscal demands of the government satisfied. Under the pressure of bad harvests and consequent debt the *colonus*—as we have seen—was apt to take refuge in flight. Consequently at some date during the third century—perhaps in consequence of a census carried out by Diocletian . . . the attachment of the tenant-farmer to the manorial estate was made enforceable at law. In a rescript of Constantine dated 30 October A.D. 332, this situation is clearly defined as already in existence; henceforward any *colonus* who fled was to be brought back in chains like a runaway slave.

Once established, the principle of compulsion in reference to land tenure grew rapidly. In the third century we still read of *inquilini*, men domiciled on the estates but free to move; but in the course of the fourth century they too were tied to the land and reduced to effective serfdom. By A.D. 400 the legal codes speak of the peasants as *servi terrae*, virtually slaves of the land on which they were born. More and more they are oppressed in the interests of their former landlords, now their masters; and a stream of legislation defines ever more closely the terms of their subjection.

Two Different Kinds of Humans

The Emperors viewed this growth in the power of the landlords with mixed feelings. It placed them in a dilemma. They might attempt to enrol the landlords in the service of the State by such regulations as that of Valens (A.D. 364–78), which made them responsible for the collection of all the taxes for which their *coloni* were liable. At the same time it was recognized that the growth of the landlords was essentially a symptom of the breakdown of the State. Everywhere the colonate was constantly being recruited from the ranks of the independent peasants, whom hard times drove to throw themselves on the mercy of the local landlord, surrendering their freedom in exchange for his patronage and protection. In A.D. 368 this practice was declared illegal by the same emperor Valens, who thus sought simultaneously to check and utilize an inevitable but ultimately disruptive institution. In fact the great landlords throve against the State and usurped its functions. Thus we find them along the northern frontiers, or in Africa, raising private armies of slaves . . . to carry out frontier defence, and expelling the barbarian alone. But in the long run, by weakening the central authority, the manorial system weakened defence too, and especially in the western provinces it accelerated the disruption of the Empire. Meanwhile it helped in the general process by which the population of the Empire crystallized into the various social classes, each with its duties carefully defined in the new body of legislation which sprang up to give full sanction to the authoritarian state.

These gradings, which form the essence of the later mediaeval world, begin to appear during the first three centuries A.D., and find their full legal authority in the fourth. The old categories of *cives Romani*, freedmen, slaves and the like, no longer exist. Instead, the whole population of the Empire is divided into *honestiores*, who include the Emperor, the (Christian) priesthood and the new landed proprietors, together with officers, civil servants and the few big families of the towns, and *humiliores*, who include ultimately everyone else, whether serf or slave, craftsman or peasant. For these two grades there are separate functions, separate privileges and separate punishments; the antagonism of the classes has once more reached its logical end in the artificial creation of two different kinds of human being.

This structure, stable, simplified and primitive, was what came out of the Empire. Under this system the legacy of the ancient world was transmitted to later times. Meanwhile the real classical world had perished in the west. At the end of the fourth century the Danubian troops were disbanded because there was no longer any paymaster; and in the fifth century it proved impossible to raise even the small armies of ten to twenty thousand men necessary to repel the barbarians. The invasions thus met with little real resistance in a world already torn within, decentralized and irreparably weakened both socially and economically. . . . Men lost faith in the Empire, in its justice and in its righteousness, even if they still assumed its continued existence as a matter of habit. We hear of men taking refuge with the barbarians, and of others who gave them aid and encouragement as they penetrated the Roman provinces. Thus a few thousand barbarians were enough to push over this tottering edifice [i.e., the crumbling Empire].

Christianity Undermined Rome's Patriotic and Military Spirit

Michael Grant

One of the major social trends of the Later Empire was the growing disunity between pagans (non-Christians) and Christians. As popular classical scholar Michael Grant explains in this insightful, well-written tract, the spread of certain Christian ideas tended to weaken the Empire's social, political, and military fabric. On the one hand, he says, many Christian bishops and writers told their followers that it was wrong for people to be soldiers or to serve the state in various other ways. On the other, Augustine and other influential late classical Christian philosophers advocated a spiritual withdrawal; that is, they preached that the Empire was destined to fall sooner or later, and that what mattered more was the heavenly rather than the earthly realm. This was bound to produce widespread apathy about the serious economic, military, and other problems the Later Empire faced.

If the pagans, and the products of their educational system, failed to meet the challenge of the crisis owing to excessively traditional attitudes, the great churchmen and theologians, men of superior brains and character who in earlier times would have been public servants, were guilty, too often, of a different but equally serious fault: that of discouraging other people from serving the state, either in a peaceful or a warlike capacity.

This had been a natural enough attitude in the old days when the state was engaged in persecuting Christianity.

Their feelings at that period were summed up by [the Christian apologist] Origen: 'We Christians defend the Empire by praying for it, soldiers in a spiritual welfare much more vital than any in which a Roman legionary serves.' In the same spirit, his more radical contemporary Tertullian argued that a Christian soldier in the Roman army who had refused to put a garland on his head during a pagan festival was entirely justified, even though his refusal might be followed by his own imprisonment, and by the persecution of his co-religionists. Indeed, the command to 'turn the other cheek', attributed to Jesus, made it difficult for a Christian to be a Roman soldier at all; and there were numerous specific instances of men who, after embracing Christianity, felt unable to serve in the army any longer.

Nor was the Christian attitude to civilian public service any more favourable. For the scriptural saying 'You cannot serve two masters, God and Mammon', was interpreted by identifying Mammon with the Emperor. 'Nothing, then, is more foreign to us than the state,' felt Tertullian. And the church Council held in about 306 at Illiberis (Elvira) in Spain declared that no member of the faith who had been appointed to an official post could be allowed to come to church throughout his entire period of office.

But it may seem somewhat surprising that, after the Empire became Christian, the church and its leaders, although they were now the partners of the Emperor, still persisted in their old conviction that Christianity was incompatible with state service. In 313, for example, the Council of Arelate (Arles) in Gaul pronounced that those who wished to take up political life were excluded from communion. For, in the words of an early papal letter to the Gauls, 'those who have acquired secular power and administered secular justice cannot be free from sin'. In consequence, a series of Popes, including Siricius and Innocent I, debarred those who had held administrative jobs from holy orders, explaining that this was because such government posts, even if not actually sinful in themselves, were gravely perilous to a man's soul all the same.

The Refusal to Fight for the State

Moreover, this veto was still specifically extended, as in earlier days, to those who had served in the army. Indeed, the Christian leaders of the time, in spite of their new and intimate associations with the government, still continued to speak out frequently and openly against military service. [The fourth-century bishop of Alexandria] Athanasius explicitly praised Christianity because it alone implanted a truly pacifist disposition, since the *only* foe it battled against was Evil. [Another bishop,] Basil of Caesarea related this attitude very rigorously to practical life, declaring that a soldier who killed a man in the course of his duties was guilty of murder and must be excommunicated. Even Pope Damasus, from his position of close alliance with the state, still praised Christian soldiers who courted martyrdom by throwing away their arms. St Martin of Tours asked to be released from the army because 'I am Christ's soldier: I am not allowed to fight'. And when taxed with cowardice, he was said to have offered to stand in front of the battle line armed only with a cross. But then, according to the legend, the enemy surrendered immediately, so that no such gesture proved necessary.

Paulinus, bishop of Nola, supported these arguments against the profession of arms in explicit detail, contrasting it with the wearing of armour for God.

> . . . Do not any longer love this world or its military service, for Scripture's authority attests that whoever is a friend of this world is an enemy of God. He who is a soldier with the sword is the servant of death, and when he sheds his own blood or that of another, this is the reward for his service.

> He will be regarded as guilty of death either because of his own death or because of his sin, because a soldier in war, fighting not so much for himself as for another, is either conquered and killed, or conquers and wins a pretext for death—for he cannot be a victor unless he first sheds blood.

For those who were defenders of the tottering fabric of society, there is not much sign of any encouragement here. It remained for the unknown fifth-century writer of *On the Calling of all Nations* to express, not merely the common belief that barbarians were the instruments of divine punishment, but the actual hope that Roman arms would *fail* against the enemy whose 'weapons which destroy the world do but promote the grace of Christianity'.

When such views were being expressed by bishops and theologians, it was hardly to be expected that their congregations would show any greater enthusiasm for the army and its tasks, however pressing these might be; and so the power of the Empire to resist its foes was sapped. Pacifism can only be pursued when no potential external enemies exist—and that was not the situation of ancient Rome.

Anticipations of the End of the World

Another menace to the loyal defence of the state was something more subtle. It came from Augustine, who possessed one of the best intellects of his own or any other age, and composed very numerous and abundant writings. Now Augustine could not accurately be described as a pacifist at all. The saying 'turn the other cheek', he pointed out, can only be regarded as metaphorical, since to take it literally would be fatal to the welfare of the state. Wars were sometimes, he believed, a grim necessity, and might even be just, and in any case Jesus never told soldiers not to serve and fight. Yet Augustine discouraged national service by more insidious means. Just as the monks undermined the Empire by physical withdrawal, so he undermined it, too, by a sort of spiritual withdrawal: the state we most urgently need to serve is not the Roman Empire, but an ideal, heavenly state.

His work, the *Civitas Dei*, rendered as the 'City of God', though the word rather means 'community' or 'society', is not primarily a political treatise, but a work of theology. Nevertheless, its abundant pages yield important evidence of Augustine's influence on the political events of his time. Plato had described an ideal city which was the forerunner of Augustine's. It was 'laid up somewhere in heaven', to be a model for actual communities upon earth. In later Greek times the Stoic philosophers had envisaged the world as a

GLADIATOR FIGHTING A LION. A MARBLE GROUP IN MUNICH, BAVARIA.

This sketch depicts a gladiator fighting a lion. The increasing numbers of Christians in the Empire condemned such brutal spectacles, and Christian leaders called on the authorities to ban them. These efforts were eventually successful.

single unit, a cosmopolis, which is itself a potential City of God on earth, since all men possess a share of the divine spark. Then another philosophical thinker, Posidonius, turned this doctrine to the advantage of the Roman Empire, which he saw as the only realizable cosmopolis.

St Paul, too, wrote that the minds of the enemies of Christ are set on earthly things, whereas Christian believers on earth 'by contrast are citizens of heaven'. Yet he held that earthly governments had to be obeyed, for they are instituted by God and are in the service of God, so that those who rebel against them are flouting divine authority. And in the same spirit the Gospels record a much-discussed saying of Jesus, 'Render to Caesar the things that are Caesar's, and to God the things that are God's'.

After the accession of Constantine, it was believed by his supporters that the words of Jesus and Paul enjoining obedience to the earthly power had become peculiarly relevant, since the unity between the heavenly and earthly communities detected by Posidonius had actually begun, under the reigning Emperor's auspices, to come about. Subsequently Theodosius I, by his total union between state and church, seemed to have completed the process, and the official doctrine was now insistent that by serving the Christian government a man was also serving heaven.

But when Alaric sacked Rome in 410, a wave of pessimism came over the relations between church and state, and it finds expression in the thought of Ambrose, Jerome and Augustine. This gloom was based on certain antique attitudes. In particular there had always been a widespread pagan doctrine that the world, so far from exhibiting modern concepts of progress, was steadily declining from the Golden Age of the past down to the Iron Age of the present, with catastrophe to come in the future. Such doctrines, which conveniently coincided with Christian views of the Day of Doom and the Last Judgment, enabled Ambrose, for example, to take a most unfavourable view of the condition and prospects of the Roman Empire. After the battle of Adrianople, he announced 'the massacre of all humanity, the end of the world', and then again in 386 he recorded 'diseases spreading, time nearing its end. We are indeed in the twilight of the world'. Christianity he saw as the crop coming just before the frosts of the winter: and the approaching world's end, as one of his followers explicitly declared, was to be preceded by the collapse of Rome. . . .

Reactions to the Sack of Rome

Upon this world of unconstructive thinking burst Alaric in 410. Almost a century earlier, the Christian writer Lactantius had said that the fall of the city of Rome would mean the end of the world, and now, with Alaric's onslaught, both these events seemed to have come at one and the same time. Although, in fact, the Visigoths only stayed for three days, and did not do as much damage as might have been expected, this blow that felled the Eternal City seemed an appalling horror to optimists and pessimists alike.

Jerome, although far away in Bethlehem, took it as hard as anyone else. Alaric's earlier invasions had already filled him with the gloomiest forebodings, and now, after the sack of the city, he wrote to other friends in desperation, almost believing that the blackest prophecies had been right, and that the last days of the world were truly come.

> . . . I dare hardly speak until I receive more definite news. For I am torn between hope and despair, tormented by the terrible things that have befallen our friends. But now that this glorious Light of the World has been tampered with—defiled; and now that, with this city, the whole world, so to speak, is faced with annihilation, 'I am dumb, and am humbled, and kept silent from good things.'

Three years later, he was still reverting to the same theme.

> . . . Terrifying news comes to us from the West. Rome has been taken by assault. Men are ransoming their lives with gold. Though despoiled, they are still hounded, so that after their goods they may pay with their very lives.

> My voice is still, and sobs disturb my every utterance. The city has been conquered which had once subjugated an entire world.

Nevertheless, the Christian view remained equivocal since Alaric, in his work of destruction, seemed to be acting as the human instrument of God, and imposing a divine visitation, punishment, and test. 'God's providence', wrote Augustine, 'constantly uses war to correct and chasten the corrupt morals of mankind, as it also uses such afflictions to train men in a righteous and laudable way of life, removing to a better state those whose life is approved, or else keeping them in this world for further service.'

Yet on hearing for the first time of the capture of Rome Augustine's first reaction, like Jerome's, had been one of deep shock. 'Tidings of terror are reaching us,' he declared to his African congregation. 'There has been a massacre: also great fires, looting, murder, torture.' Later he realized that these first reports were overstated. Acting with relative restraint, Alaric, himself a Christian, had spared the personnel and property of the church.

The Heavenly and Earthly Cities

However, many people, and not only pagans, were asking why, since the Imperial government was Christian and allegedly enjoyed God's backing, had God allowed such a thing to happen. Nothing so frightful had ever occurred under pagan rule. It was in order to meet this challenge that Augustine began to write the twenty two books of the *City of God*. 'The first five', explains its author, 'refute those who attribute prosperity and adversity to the cult of pagan gods or to the prohibition of this cult. The next five are against those who hold that ills are never wanting to men, but that worship of the pagan gods helps towards the future life after death.' The second part of the work contains twelve books. The first four describe the birth of the two cities, one of God, the other of the world. The second four continue their story, and the third four depict their final destiny. These last twelve books contain a far-reaching philosophy of history which does not depend solely on Alaric's capture of Rome but possesses a universal application.

Augustine had read Plato's *Republic* in Latin translations, and had studied commentaries on the work. But he borrowed the concept of the two cities from certain contemporary North-African Christians, the Donatists . . ., who held that one city served God and his loyal angels, while the other worked for the Devil and his rebel angels and demons. At present, it was true, the two cities seemed inextricably mixed together within the church as in the rest of the world, but at the Last Judgment they would appear in manifest separation, one on God's left and the other on his right, like the captor city Babylon and its liberated captive Jerusalem.

This vision of captivity and liberation excited Augustine and inspired him. And in consequence, during the year following 410, he began to develop this whole theme for his readers and congregations, elaborating it with the passion of a masterly and persuasive artist. Two loves, he says, have created two cities: love of God the heavenly city, to the contempt of self; love of self the earthly city, to the contempt of God. The city of God is the city of the righteous, which contains God and his angels and saints in heaven, and all men and women who lead good lives on earth. The earthly city contains all un-righteous men and women wherever they be in the universe—fallen angels, the souls of the unrighteous, the unrighteous in the world. Although, therefore, marginal points of contact exist, the earthly city is *not the same* as the Roman Empire.

What, then, does Augustine think of that Empire? His an-swer is founded on his doctrine of Grace. Without this god-given help to human beings, he feels that we who are lumps of perdition—sinful ever since Adam's Fall—can never attain eternal salvation. Augustine's own recurrent struggles be-tween the flesh and the spirit caused him to share St Paul's poor opinion of what a person can achieve by his own un-aided will, and made him break with the more optimistic, classical, humanist view that we can achieve great things by our own endeavours.

The Human Will Versus God's Will

Augustine's attitude incurred the intense disapproval and anger of another Christian theologian of the day. This was Pelagius. Of British or Irish extraction, he came to Rome as a monk about 400. Like others, he was horrified by Alaric's sack of Rome, when 'the mistress of the world shivered, crushed with fear, at the sound of the blaring trumpets and the howling of the Goths'.

But Pelagius' reaction to such disasters was by no means limited to fatalistic gloom and despair. Both before and after the capture of the city, he found himself deeply dissatisfied with the moral sluggishness of many prosperous people of Rome. In an attempt to raise their easygoing standards, he insisted on a strenuous individual endeavour to attain salva-tion. He was convinced that the barrier of corruption which keeps original innocence and goodness out of our reach is insubstantial, and can be overcome by a bracing effort: we sin by a *voluntary* imitation of Adam, and an equally volun-tary decision can cast our sins behind us.

The salvation to which Pelagius primarily referred was not of this world. Yet his doctrine was obviously applicable to worldly salvation as well—to the rehabilitation of the fail-ing Roman Empire. If people bestirred themselves more and tried harder, it could be deduced from Pelagius, they would be better men. And that also meant, though he did not put it in such a way, that they would be better able to come to the rescue of their country. . . .

Learning of this insistence upon the basic soundness and effectiveness of the human will, Augustine revolted against Pelagius even more violently than Pelagius had revolted against Augustine. He accused Pelagius of teaching, 'like the philosophers of the pagans', that man by his own unassisted free will could achieve goodness without any help from God at all. Probably the criticism was unjustified, since what Pelagius really wanted to say was that heaven helps those who help themselves. But Augustine persisted in his censures for many years and wrote a treatise, *On Free Will*, endeavouring to strike what he felt to be a more pious balance between men's limited capacity for autonomous enterprise and his dependence on the divine power. . . .

The doctrine of Pelagius was of greater value—on the practical plane of daily events and emergencies—to the later Roman Empire. . . . His doctrine of the will at least wanted people to *try*. Augustine's philosophy, on the other hand, led to fatalism. Yet his incomparable eloquence, ably supported by many other preachers, ensured that it was his view which ultimately prevailed.

So Pelagius was doomed to failure. Jerome called him a fat hound weighed down by Scotch porridge, and he twice suffered excommunication. When and where he died is unknown. But after his death, the controversy continued with unabated vigour, and the Gallic monks and theologians felt considerable sympathy with his views, for Augustine's increasingly vehement assertions of Grace as man's only hope seemed to undermine human effort.

The Empire Destined to Fall?

Indeed, his pronouncements also carried more fundamental political implications, affecting the whole concept of the Roman Empire. For since man, he concluded, is so totally corrupted by the fall of Adam that he is bound at some time to sin, and even Grace cannot prevent this inevitable outcome; since, that is to say, for as long as he lives, he can never cease to be flawed, then all his institutions are flawed as well. Even the church, though it provides the only bridge to the heavenly city, remains a mixture of good wheat and bad weeds. How much more imperfect, then, must be the state, the Roman Empire itself!

True, although often perverted by evil wills, it is a natural and a divine necessity which God granted to the Romans. By his ordinance, continued Augustine, there is a king for temporal life, as there is a king for eternal life. Earthly rulers have special services they can render to God, just because they are rulers. . . .

When such men rule, one can see 'a faint shadowy resemblance between the Roman Empire and the heavenly city'. The state, in fact, has its uses. Love of our neighbour, felt Augustine, makes our patriotic and civic duties obligatory. Soldiers, rulers, and judges alike have to stay at their posts. And yet, all the same, we are reading the thoughts of a man in whom national feeling is so strictly and totally subordinated to religious considerations that it can hardly, in any meaningful sense, be said to exist.

From the nationalist sentiments which had defended the frontiers of ancient Rome for so many centuries we have travelled a vast distance. For example, while granting that wars can be just and even necessary, Augustine concludes that their 'victories bring death with them or are doomed to death', and the vast extent of Rome's Empire, he adds, has given rise to every sort of detestable foreign and civil war. Augustine even says he would have preferred a number of small nations living in peace to the monolithic Empire of the Romans. 'Without justice', he declares, 'governments are merely great bands of brigands'—gangsterism on a massive scale. But 'without justice' is precisely what, in the very nature of things, these states inevitably were: and what Rome could not fail to be.

And so he preached, as others had preached before him, that 'we do not want to have dealings with the powers that be'. That is frank: it is a call to withhold service from the government. Equally frank is his reminder that the Empire is bound to collapse anyway. 'If heaven and earth are to pass away, why is it surprising if at some time the state is going to come to a stop?—if what God has made will one day vanish, then surely what Romulus made will disappear much sooner.' Even the current identification of church and state will not, cannot, suffice to stop the rot.

The State No Longer Matters

Where does all this leave the individual citizen? Rome, for his benefit, has been firmly cut down to size. Our *real*, permanent fatherland, he is told—the only true kingdom, according to the strictest idea of what is right—is elsewhere altogether. 'What we want', states Augustine, 'is a way to help us to re-turn to *that* kingdom: that is how we shall bring our sorrows to an end.' As for all the earthly crises and catastrophes, they can just be ignored—or even welcomed, seeing that God has sent them as a discipline. The calamities of a country in which you are merely a foreigner do not really affect your interests at all. When, therefore, such calamities appear, just treat them as an invitation to concentrate your desires on things eternal: and rejoice that your treasure is in a place where no enemy has the power to approach. To a patriotic pagan, disturbed by the disasters that have befallen Rome, Augustine spells out the message: 'Please pardon us if *our* country, up above, has to cause trouble to yours . . . you would acquire still greater merit if you served a higher fatherland.'

Those are not words that will impel a man to the defence of the falling Roman Empire. Augustine has shifted the cen-tre of gravity so that the state is now a good deal less than half of what matters: far from helping his country to survive, his attitude contributed to its downfall. . . .

Although Augustine's full influence was not exerted for generations to come, subsequent writers during the last years of the Western Roman Empire were already echoing his fatalistic attitude. For example, it was perhaps now that the poet Commodianus positively gloated over the downfall of the city: 'She who bragged that she was eternal now weeps to eternity.' And in the words of Orientius, bishop of Ausci . . . in south-west France, 'why go over the funeral ceremonies of a world falling into ruins, in accordance with the common law of all that passes away?' Moreover, Orosius, whom Augustine commissioned to write a history of Rome, not only reminds us once again that Rome deserved the German onslaughts—because in earlier days it had persecuted the Christians—but that these attacks will actually be beneficial, 'although this may involve the crumbling of our Empire'. Presbyter Salvian, who believed the same, added two realistic comments. First, the Empire was *already* dead, or breathing its last. Secondly, most Romans lacked the imagination to realize the supreme peril they were in: and if they did happen to possess such discernment, they lacked the nerve to do anything about it.

For the existence of this inertia—which is a very accurate diagnosis—the suggestion of Augustine that human endeavour could be of no consequence, either in this situation or any other, bore a share of the blame; or at least he very accurately represented a prevailing feeling which fell all too readily into line with the numerous other tendencies conspiring to bring about Rome's fall.

The Army Became
Undisciplined and Ineffective

Pat Southern and Karen R. Dixon

One of the main contributing factors to the disintegration
of the western Roman Empire was the steady deterioration of its army in its last century. Simply put, the military
was eventually inadequate to the task of defending the
realm, which as a result quite literally fell apart. Scholars
Pat Southern and Karen R. Dixon, both of the University
of Newcastle upon Tyne, provide this informative analysis
of the imperial army's decline. Citing various ancient writers, including Ammianus (fourth-century Latin), Vegetius
(late fourth-century Latin), Zosimus (early fifth-century
Greek), and Eugippus (fifth-century Latin), they examine
several causes for this decline. Among these are the steady
barbarization of the military ranks and an increasing lack
of resources to pay and equip the soldiers. Perhaps most
telling of all, after the huge battles fought at Adrianople
(in Thrace, in 378) and the Frigidus River (northeast of
Italy, in 394), most of the soldiers in subsequent generations were poorly trained.

It look three years of fighting before Theodosius brought
the Goths to terms in 382, when he allowed them to settle
in Thrace. The treaty which he made with them has not always been viewed in a favourable light, either by his con-
temporaries or by modern scholars, who censure Theodosius for his leniency towards the Goths. They were settled
on the very lands they had ravaged, unsupervised by the Romans and permitted to live according to their own laws. . . .
The text of Theodosius's treaty (*foedus*) of 382 is un-

known, and therefore the terms of military service exacted from the Goths also remain unknown. The exploitation of barbarian manpower was not unusual, but it seems that the terms laid down in the negotiations of 382 departed from normal practice. Before it can be stated how these terms differed, it is necessary to enquire what constituted normal practice. Usually, after the conclusion of a war, a treaty was made stipulating that the enemy should contribute a number of men to the Roman army, either *en masse* and annually thereafter, or by some similar arrangement. It was at one and the same time a means of removing potentially dangerous young men, of increasing the size of the army, and of gradually Romanizing the barbarians. The soldiers raised in this way could be distributed among existing units, thus diluting their barbarian influence, or they could be kept together, organized and trained as a regular unit, and sent to distant provinces to reduce the likelihood of their deserting to the enemy if rebellion should break out. This sort of treaty was made with tribes who remained outside the Empire and was a time-honoured method of raising men for the army.

Wholesale immigration of tribesmen into the Empire was a matter demanding a different response. Sometimes defeated tribesmen *(dediticii)* were settled inside the Empire in fairly large numbers. Other groups of barbarians entered voluntarily. Tribes had clamoured to be allowed to cross the frontiers since the Empire came into being, and had sometimes been admitted and given lands. . . . Under Augustus 50,000 Getae settled in Moesia; Tiberius allowed 40,000 Germans into Gaul and the Rhineland; Marcus Aurelius received 3000 Naristae into the Empire; Probus admitted 100,000 Bastarnae and Constantine settled 300,000 Sarmatians on lands in Thrace, Italy and Macedonia. The numbers are . . . suspect, but they serve to illustrate the magnitude of the problem. In the late Empire the numbers of barbarians seeking admission dramatically increased. . . .

Who Were the Barbarian "Federates"?

The employment of barbarians from beyond the frontiers, by means of an alliance with a tribal leader or a client king, had always been accepted as a method of increasing the size of the army for campaigns. Such troops fought under their own leaders, attached to the army for the duration of the war, then on the conclusion of peace they would return to their homes. On occasion, they might be recruited into the regular army to fill gaps in the ranks, or sometimes whole bands of them might be transformed into regular units, but most often they remained outside the army. Their chiefs would normally be strongly supported by Rome, sometimes subsidized, and kept in power in order to ensure that the frontiers were protected at least in part by tribes who had every reason to be on friendly terms with the Empire.

The term *foederati* ["federates"] is not an easily definable one, since it covers several different kinds of troops. In the late Empire, it denoted troops raised from barbarians settled within the frontiers as well as those raised from outside. The practice of settling barbarians by treaty arrangement on lands inside the Empire became more common from the end of the third century, when many frontier areas were devastated. Such settlements were widespread and frequent. . . .

Foederati could also describe conglomerations of men, not all of the same ethnic background, who had gathered around a leader. The bands of Goths following Alaric probably contained an ethnic mixture of different tribesmen. There can be no direct link with the original Goths who crossed the frontier in 376. . . . [Was] Alaric leading a nation or something more properly described as an army[?]

The distinctions between these *foederati* and the *bucellarii* are probably blurred. *Bucellarii* were private armies composed of retainers of a powerful . . . general like Stilicho. . . . The men who joined these private armies perhaps did so because their particular leader could guarantee them long-term employment.

Whatever their origin, the *foederati* attached to the army would be answerable to the Roman high command, but like the earlier *foederati*, their immediate commanders would be their own leaders. They were not part of the regular army.

By the sixth century, the *foederati* in the eastern army were quite different. These were regular troops, paid, trained and disciplined, like the rest of the army. The change presumably came about at some unknown date in the fifth century. These units were recruited exclusively from barbarians at first, then in the sixth century Romans were also admitted. . . .

In addition to individual recruitment of tribesmen to fill gaps in existing units, enrollment of large groups of barbarians in the army had been common practice since the early Empire. Marcus Aurelius used Germans to fight against Germans. . . . Claudius II enrolled Goths after defeating them. . . . Constantine's army at the battle of the Milvian Bridge was full of Germans, Gauls and Britons. . . .

The barbarian soldiers were, with few exceptions, loyal to Rome, and served her well. There was little sense of nationality among the Germanic tribes, and no unity, so that the dichotomy which modern readers might read into the labels German and Roman did not necessarily exist for the men who signed up for 20–25 years' service. Although the numbers of barbarians in the army may have seemed excessive, the cultural and moral superiority of the Romans ensured their subjection. The settlements of tribesmen were supervised by Roman officials, usually called *praepositi*, and the barbarians in the army were under the command of Roman, or thoroughly Romanized, officers. The Germans who attained positions of authority in the army and in civilian office were more Roman than the Romans, attuned to Roman civilization and ways of life.

Eastern and Western Responses to Barbarization

The process of barbarization of the army was already well under way by the time Theodosius made his treaty with the Goths, and the settlement of groups of tribesmen on Roman soil was nothing new. The crucial factor in the settlement of 382 concerns the status of the Goths, and their obligation to provide soldiers. Whereas other tribes inside the Empire were subject to Roman supervision and to Roman law, the Goths were governed by their own chiefs, and were therefore more or less autonomous. . . .

In the eastern Empire, the Gothic threat was dealt with summarily on more than one occasion. Immediately after the Roman defeat at Adrianople, sealed orders went out to the commanders of the eastern troops to summon the Goths in the army to a pay parade, and then to put them all to death. . . . Further purges of the army were carried out in 386 when another group of Goths were massacred at Tomi, and there was more slaughter after the revolt of Gainas in Constantinople. . . . Thereafter, in an attempt to reduce the proportions of Germanic tribesmen in the army, the eastern army began to recruit from the indigenous population, especially from the hardy tribes of Isaurians. It did not prove possible to maintain the army without recruitment of barbarians, but the numbers were kept small and more easily controlled. As mentioned above, by the sixth century troops with the title *foederati*, raised from barbarian tribes, were part of the regular army, subject to the same discipline as all other troops.

For some time the eastern army was weakened, since by purging it of the Goths, some of the best fighting elements had been removed. Fortunately, the Huns were temporarily defeated, albeit with great difficulty, in 408–9, and Theodosius also managed to resolve the Persian question. There were only two wars on the eastern frontier in 421–2 and 441–2, so that the government was able to concentrate on the defence of the Danube. . . . Territorially, the east was not so difficult to defend as the west. This gave the eastern emperors an opportunity to build up a dual system of defence, utilizing both the army and clever diplomacy . . . which the Byzantines developed into an art.

The western army did not find it so easy to meet the barbarian challenge by purging itself of undesirable elements. When an attempt was made to do so, the timing was faulty. On 13 August 408, the Romans in Honorius' court massacred the Germans among the Emperor's followers, and finally sacrificed Stilicho, to their immediate disadvantage. However dubious his motives may have been, Stilicho was a capable general, and the soldiers would follow him. By removing him and also weakening the army at the wrong time, the western Roman court found itself almost defenceless. The respite granted to the east did not occur in the west, and there were fewer opportunities for indigenous recruitment. When Alaric sacked Rome, the necessity of coming to terms with him meant that the anti-German elements of the court had to be silenced. . . . The western army never ceased to recruit barbarians, and never succeeded in removing them as the east had done. All that could be achieved was to preclude barbarians from the high commands. On the other hand, and perhaps more significantly, although the Western Empire accommodated the barbarians, it failed to assimilate them properly, and with this vacillating state of affairs it sealed its own doom.

A Shortage of Trained Manpower

Barbarization alone does not wholly explain the changes in the army which were detectable to fourth- and fifth-century authors, but the concomitant factors which resulted from the process were harmful. After Adrianople, and then the battle of the Frigidus, there was an urgent need to rebuild

---

The Army Had Become Contemptible

In this excerpt from his noted study of the decline of the Roman army in the fourth and fifth centuries, scholar Arther Ferrill makes the point that using traditional battlefield tactics did not help soldiers who lacked the training to execute such moves effectively.

How the mighty have fallen! One hundred years earlier the Roman army had been the most efficient fighting force on the face of the earth. By the time of Attila it was so contemptible it could be ignored in actual combat. In fact, of course, Roman troops contributed to the victory at Châlons [where Attila was defeated in 451], mainly by seizing high ground at the outset of battle, but the passages [of ancient writers] . . . offer a fascinating commentary on the fate of the Roman army in the fifth century. Despite the impact of barbarization, Roman forces continued to fight according to traditional Roman tactics, yet those tactics, previously so superior, seemed absurd to the barbarians of the fifth century.

the armies of east and west. The two armies did not completely disappear, but when they were eventually reconstructed, it could be said that most of the links with the Roman armies of the past had been severed. It was not necessarily a question of shortage of manpower; it was a shortage of trained manpower, which is vastly different. This is one of the reasons why the apparent recovery after the disastrous battles of the late fourth century was not as effective as, for example, the seemingly effortless recovery after the loss of two expeditionary armies in the Dacian campaigns under Domitian [in the first century]. Military disasters had occurred in the early Empire without leading to collapse, and ravaged lands had been restored, but that was before the decades of exhaustion that the late Empire had experienced without respite.

The sources are deceptive. The poems of Ausonius and the letters of Sidonius attest to a reasonably settled life in late Roman Gaul, given that the circumstances were not

---

What must have happened is reasonably clear. To fight effectively in close order, troops require intensive drill and rigorous discipline. Romans of the fifth century apparently maintained the old formations but abandoned the necessary training. As a result they combined the worst features of the Roman and barbarian styles of fighting. Close formation and indiscipline make a very sad conjunction. Troops not drilled to fight in formation should not try to do so. Without intensive training the looser formations of the barbarians (who did not try to maintain a rigid line) are actually a better use of manpower. In the East, Byzantine emperors—less influenced by federate barbarian units—maintained a firmer discipline and drill, resulting in the superb army of Belisarius in the sixth century under Justinian. As the emperors and generalissimos of the West relied more and more heavily on federates, the traditional Roman army of the West simply disintegrated.

Arther Ferrill, *The Fall of the Roman Empire: The Military Explanation*. New York: Thames and Hudson, 1986, pp. 152–53.

ideal. But the recovery of Gaul after the ravages of the Frankish and Alamannic raids was probably far from complete. Similarly neither east nor west fully recovered from the effects of Adrianople and the Frigidus. The army had diminished in public esteem, as indicated by the marked reluctance of most men to serve in it. . . . This reluctance among Romans meant that the soldiers were mostly barbarians on both sides whenever so-called Roman armies clashed in civil wars, but Roman tradition, discipline, training and fighting methods had not yet been entirely extinguished in the early 370s. . . . At the end of the fourth century this changed, and the process of decline already apparent in the army took a firmer hold, making it impossible to reverse the trends towards complete barbarization. . . .

The law codes bear witness to the measures to which Theodosius was driven to refurbish troops from 378 onwards. Many of the laws were designed to unmask those who sought to avoid military service by one method or another. In 380, there was an effort to enforce the rule that sons of veterans must enlist. . . . Then there were penalties for those who offered slaves for the army instead of suitable recruits . . . and stronger measures against men who mutilated themselves to avoid service. In order to discourage the practice, it was declared that two mutilated men would be taken in place of one whole one. . . . By 406, all scruples about the unsuitability of slaves had been abandoned in the west, and the emperors were calling them to arms. . . .

It may have seemed that the shortages of manpower could be solved instantly by filling the ranks of the army with barbarians and by negotiating with various allied chieftains for temporary contingents of tribesmen to fight in specific wars. But the losses of Adrianople were not to be counted simply in numerical terms of manpower. What had been lost were experienced men, disciplined and trained to Roman standards. If, in the past, it had always proved possible to rebuild the army systematically and methodically, the situation now was too precarious and the danger too widespread to allow for anything other than rapid, piecemeal responses, which differed in each half of the Empire.

The Eastern Empire conducted its successive purges and endangered itself by reducing the size of its army, but it survived by a combination of good fortune and good management, and remained Roman by tradition even if it became Oriental in fact. Its territory was more homogeneous and easier to defend, and even though it was bordered by the Persian Empire, the threat posed by this sophisticated enemy did not cause the disintegration that the barbarians caused in the west.

The Western emperors never appointed a German *magister militum* after the removal of Stilicho. With the exception of Ulfilas and Sigisvult, who were Goths, after 408 all the *magistri* were Romans. But if the high-ranking officers were no longer barbarians, the troops were still recruited from tribesmen. The West retained an effective army under Aetius, but its lack of Romanization became more and more apparent. . . . Barbarians were not naturally disciplined. . . . It was unusual that the barbarians stayed at their posts, did not pillage and loot, and did not cause confusion. Ammianus had no very elevated opinion of barbarians; in scattered references . . . he describes them as inhuman and vicious, using all the stock epithets. With more insight from a military point of view, he says they are discouraged by the slightest set-back, disorganized, incapable of following any coherent plan, and unable to foresee a train of events. In other words, they were thoroughly unmilitary from a Roman point of view.

Zosimus has another point to add, which may concern only one army at one particular time, but is none the less deeply significant. He says that no record was kept of those enrolled in the army, and the deserters whom Theodosius had reinstated could go home whenever they felt like it, substituting other men in their places. Granted that modern armies are much more highly trained in various special tasks than was the Roman army, chaos would have resulted if, for instance, a tank driver in Normandy in 1944 had decided to go home, substituting the nearest garage mechanic to do his job for a few months. Such a lack of central control and lapse of disciplinary standards was nothing less than disastrous. Combined with the lack of a cadre of trained men to hand down tradition, and the lack of active training to remedy this defect, the downward spiral accelerated alarmingly and could not be stopped. . . .

In these circumstances the process of training and of Romanization could not operate. Lack of training would cause irreparable harm in a very short time. . . . With the disappearance of discipline and training, Roman combat methods also disappeared as a matter of course. It can be no accident that Vegetius, in the very first chapter after his preface and fulsome dedication, perhaps to Theodosius I, points out that it was discipline and training which enabled the Roman armies to conquer all peoples. He goes on to say that 'a small force, highly trained, is more likely to win battles than a raw and untrained horde'. . . .

Training is eased when there is a cadre of experienced soldiers round which to build up each unit, so that the original ethnic background of the new recruits is hardly of any significance. Romanization of tribesmen in the army is similarly eased when Roman culture is in the ascendancy. Neither of these elements applied after the battles of Adrianople and the Frigidus, and the situation was compounded by other serious factors. . . . At a time when both dynamic commanders and lots of money were needed, the Roman Empire had neither. If the army could have been Romanized and trained as it had been in the early Empire, the Western Empire may have survived longer. But the procedure for training an army and for Romanization of the barbarians required a commodity which was never granted to the west: time.

The Army Eventually Ceases to Exist

The break-up when it came proceeded rapidly, from the first decade of the fifth century. The inability of the western government to defend the Empire arose from lack of centralized administrative control and impoverishment of resources. Civil wars between usurpers accelerated the decline. Constantius II withdrew troops from Britain in 407; three years later Honorius decided against trying to regain the island. The army was withdrawn from Spain in 411. The Western Empire shrank to a shadow of its former self. Italy was naturally the first priority, the second was Gaul, virtually the only other province that was defended. Even the Rhine frontier was allowed to be overrun. The *magister militum* Aetius, though a Roman, had been a hostage among the Huns, and increasingly used these ties of loyalty to recruit Huns for his army, with which he successfully fought Burgundians and Visigoths in Gaul. Appeals for help from the other provinces were ignored. . . .

The exact date when the Western Empire ceased to exist is hard to ascertain. There are successive stages, all equally qualified for the honour, but even after the widely accepted date of 476, Roman forms of law and military institutions were not completely dead, surviving as they did in the barbarian kingdoms. The date at which the western Roman army ceased to exist is no less problematic. There was no formal disbandment centrally directed from Ravenna or Rome. It could be said that even the soldiers serving in the army were not really sure of their demise as an institution. A famous passage from Eugippius' *Vita Sancti Severini* best illustrates this. He describes how, while the Romans were in power, soldiers were maintained in many towns at public expense to guard the frontier. But when this custom ceased, several whole units of soldiers disappeared. The men at Batava (modern Passau, at the junction of the rivers Inn and Danube) remained at their posts, and sent a delegation to Italy to find out why they had received no pay. Some days later, their bodies floated down-river and came to rest on the banks, silent testimony to the end of Rome's ability to keep her Empire intact and to defend her frontiers.

The Barbarians Overran the Western Empire

J.B. Bury

In this excerpt from his famous history of the Later Empire, the late distinguished historian J.B. Bury accepts the fact that Rome's western sector disintegrated because numerous groups of Germanic tribal peoples steadily overran it. However, he argues, this scenario had no major overriding cause, nor was it by any means inevitable, as some scholars have suggested. Instead, says Bury, the barbarians were ultimately successful because of a series of contingent events, almost all of which hurt rather than helped the situation. In others words, one unfortunate event was not followed by a fortunate one, but rather by another unfortunate one; and this downward spiral continued until the damage was too extensive to repair.

The explanations of the calamities of the Empire which have been hazarded by modern writers are of a different order from those which occurred to witnesses of the events, but they are not much more satisfying. The illustrious historian whose name will always be associated with the "Decline" of the Roman Empire [i.e., Edward Gibbon] invoked "the principle of decay," a principle which has itself to be explained. Depopulation, the Christian religion, [and] the fiscal system have all been assigned as causes of the Empire's decline in strength. If these or any or them were responsible for its dismemberment by the barbarians in the West, it may be asked how it was that in the East, where the same causes operated, the Empire survived much longer intact and united.

Excerpted from *History of the Later Roman Empire, 395–565*, by J.B. Bury. Reprinted with permission from Dover Publications, Inc.

Sheer Numbers of People?

Consider depopulation. The depopulation of Italy was an important fact and it had far-reaching consequences. But it was a process which had probably reached its limit in the time of Augustus. There is no evidence that the Empire was less populous in the fourth and fifth centuries than in the first. The "sterility of the human harvest" in Italy and Greece affected the history of the Empire from its very beginning, but does not explain the collapse in the fifth century. The truth is that there are two distinct questions which have been confused. It is one thing to seek the causes which changed the Roman State from what it was in the best days of the Republic to what it had become in the age of Theodosius the Great—a change which from certain points of view may be called a "decline." It is quite another thing to ask why the State which could resist its enemies on many frontiers in the days of Diocletian and Constantine and Julian suddenly gave way in the days of Honorius. "Depopulation" may partly supply the answer to the first question, but it is not an answer to the second. Nor can the events which transferred the greater part of western Europe to German masters be accounted for by the numbers of the peoples who invaded it. The notion of vast hosts of warriors, numbered by hundreds of thousands, pouring over the frontiers, is . . . perfectly untrue. The total number of one of the large East German nations probably seldom exceeded 100,000, and its army of fighting men can rarely have been more than from 20,000 to 30,000. They were not a deluge, overwhelming and irresistible, and the Empire had a well-organised military establishment at the end of the fourth century, fully sufficient in capable hands to beat them back. As a matter of fact, since the defeat at Hadrianople which was due to the blunders of Valens, no very important battle was won by Germans over Imperial forces during the whole course or the invasions.

Christianity a Disintegrating Force?

It has often been alleged that Christianity in its political effects was a disintegrating force and tended to weaken the power of Rome to resist her enemies. It is difficult to see that it had any such tendency, so long as the Church itself was united. Theological heresies were indeed to prove a disintegrating force in the East in the seventh century, when differences in doctrine which had alienated the Christians in Egypt and Syria from the government of Constantinople facilitated the conquests of the Saracens. But . . . there was no such vital or deep-reaching division in the West, and the effect of Christianity was to unite, not to sever, to check, rather than to emphasise, national or sectional feeling. In the political calculations of Constantine it was probably this ideal of unity, as a counterpoise to the centrifugal tendencies which had been clearly revealed in the third century, that was the great recommendation of the religion which he raised to power. Nor is there the least reason to suppose that Christian teaching had the practical effect of making men less loyal to the Empire or less ready to defend it. The Christians were as pugnacious as the pagans. Some might read Augustine's *City of God* with edification, but probably very few interpreted its theory with such strict practical logic as to be indifferent to the safety of the Empire. Hardly the author himself, though this has been disputed. . . .

One Event Led to Another

The truth is that the success of the barbarians in penetrating and founding states in the western provinces cannot be explained by any general considerations. It is accounted for by the actual events and would be clearer if the story were known more fully. The gradual collapse of the Roman power in this section of the Empire was the consequence of *a series of contingent events.* No general causes can be assigned that made it inevitable.

The first contingency was the irruption of the Huns into Europe, an event resulting from causes which were quite independent of the weakness or strength of the Roman Empire. It drove the Visigoths into the Illyrian provinces, and the difficult situation was unhappily mismanaged. One Emperor was defeated and lost his life; it was his own fault. That disaster, which need not have occurred, was a second contingency. His successor allowed a whole federate nation to settle on provincial soil; he took the line of least resistance

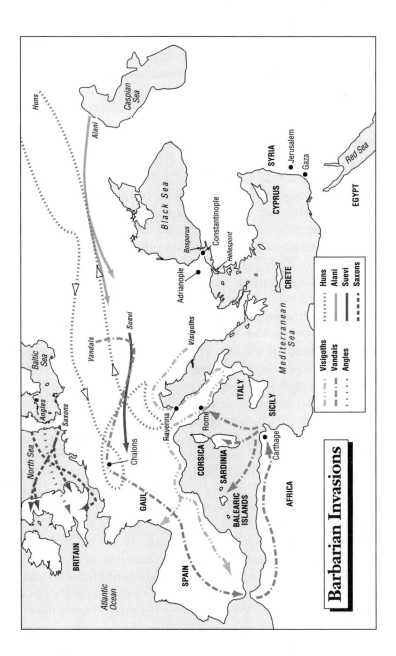

Barbarian Invasions

and established an unfortunate precedent. He did not foresee consequences which, if he had lived ten or twenty years longer, might not have ensued. His death was a third contingency. But the situation need have given no reason for grave alarm if the succession had passed to an Emperor like himself, or Valentinian I, or even Gratian. Such a man was not procreated by Theodosius and the government of the West was inherited by a feeble-minded boy. That was a fourth event, dependent on causes which had nothing to do with the condition of the Empire.

In themselves these events need not have led to disaster. If the guardian of Honorius and director of his government had been a man of Roman birth and tradition, who commanded the public confidence, a man such as Honorius himself was afterwards to find in Constantius and his successor in Aetius, all might have been tolerably well. But there was a point of weakness in the Imperial system, the practice of elevating Germans to the highest posts of command in the army. It had grown up under Valentinian I, Gratian, and Theodosius; it had led to the rebellion of Maximus, and had cost Valentinian II his life. The German in whom Theodosius reposed his confidence and who assumed the control of affairs on his death probably believed that he was serving Rome faithfully, but it was a singular misfortune that at a critical moment when the Empire had to be defended not only against Germans without but against a German nation which had penetrated inside, the responsibility should have devolved upon a German. Stilicho [the half-Vandal Roman general who wielded great power as Honorius's regent] did not intend to be a traitor, but his policy was as calamitous as if he had planned deliberate treachery. For it meant civil war. The dissatisfaction of the Romans in the West was expressed in the rebellion of Constantine, the successor of Maximus, and if Stilicho had had his way the soldiers of Honorius and of Arcadius would have been killing one another for the possession of Illyricum. When he died the mischief was done; Goths had Italy at their mercy, Gaul and Spain were overrun by other peoples. His Roman successors could not undo the results of events which need never have happened.

Rome's Fall Not Inevitable

The supremacy of a Stilicho was due to the fact that the defence of the Empire had come to depend on the enrolment of barbarians, in large numbers, in the army, and that it was necessary to render the service attractive to them by the prospect of power and wealth. This was, of course, a consequence of the decline in military spirit, and of depopulation, in the old civilised Mediterranean countries. . . . Yet this policy need not have led to the dismemberment of the Empire, and but for that series of chances its western provinces would not have been converted, as and when they were, into German kingdoms. It may be said that a German penetration of western Europe must ultimately have come about. But even if that were certain, it might have happened in another way, at a later time, more gradually, and with less violence. The point of the present contention is that Rome's loss of her provinces in the fifth century was not an "inevitable effect of any of those features which have been rightly or wrongly described as causes or consequences of her general 'decline.'" The central fact that Rome could not dispense with the help of barbarians for her wars . . . may be held to be the cause of her calamities, but it was a weakness which might have continued to be far short of fatal but for the sequence of contingencies pointed out above.

Rome's Decline Helped Ensure the Triumph of Western Civilization

Chester G. Starr

In this thought-provoking essay, renowned University of Michigan scholar Chester G. Starr concludes first, that no single explanation for the fall of the western Roman Empire satisfactorily explains that great turning point. What is perhaps more important to consider, he suggests, is how the fall of Rome affected future ages. In this view, the end of ancient times in Europe, though on the surface *de*structive, was in certain other ways *con*structive; for in the upheavals attending the transition from ancient to medieval times were planted the seeds for the eventual rise and global triumph of western Europe.

Across Eurasia the period from A.D. 300 to 700 . . . brought tremendous changes. If we compare it with that earlier upheaval which occurred in the centuries centering on 1000 B.C., the dimensions of the Germanic and Hunnic invasions shrink; for they nowhere cut the inherited threads of civilization as ruthlessly as did the invaders who brought the fall of the Minoan-Mycenaean world, of the Hittite empire, and (somewhat earlier) of the Indus civilization.

Nevertheless the centuries after A.D. 300 formed a dismal era for many peoples, a great turning point which must be termed the end of the ancient world. The change did not take place everywhere at the same time or with the same intensity; the history of Eurasia cannot be compressed into facile [easy] patterns of uniformity. Yet whether one explores in detail the history of modern China, of modern India, or

Excerpted from *A History of the Ancient World*, by Chester G. Starr. Copyright ©1991 by Oxford University Press, Inc. Reprinted with permission from Oxford University Press, Inc.

of modern Europe, the story after this period is distinctly different from that which lay before.

Why, then, did the change take place? And exactly what is its meaning in the long development of human history? Questions of this nature are so sweeping that they can have no pat answers; they are, indeed, upsetting questions even to pose. Yet each responsible historian is obligated to set down his own interpretation, when queried; but in doing so he must seek to provide his interrogator with food for thought and disagreement. To narrow the field for greater precision, let us turn back to the western provinces of the Roman Empire, the area from which modern European civilization has sprung and also the district which suffered most severely in the end of the ancient world.

A Diversity of Explanations

Throughout the Middle Ages men in western Europe felt themselves directly linked to Rome—a significant fact in itself in suggesting the fundamental continuity between ancient and medieval. Rome, however, they visualized in terms of the Later Empire, as preserved in Justinian's [law] code and in the organization of the church. During the Renaissance of the fourteenth and fifteenth centuries, scholars, artists, and despots came to glorify the earlier Caesars, and citizens of such free cities as Florence even at times appreciated some of the qualities of the Republic. As men thus looked back, they began to realize there had been a break, and the term "medieval" was soon coined.

Once the modern world decided that there had been a "Decline and Fall of the Roman Empire," as Edward Gibbon entitled his great study, it sought to explain why this lugubrious [dismal] interruption of civilization—as the modern western world egotistically measured the event—had occurred. An historian can gain both profit and amusement from surveying the bewildering diversity of explanations which have been seriously advanced.

Some scholars fix on a mechanical or external cause, independent of human foresight, for example, exhaustion of the soil, the rise of malaria, plague (as under Marcus Aurelius), changes in climate, or even the Germanic invasions themselves. Others seek an evil person or bad policy, such as the unworthy emperor Commodus (180–92), or the loss of power by the old upper classes in the third or fourth centuries. Others still slip off into truly mystical explanations by talking of the "victory of the Orient," that is, the purported conquest of Greco-Roman rationality by Oriental faith; by emphasizing an assumed foundation of the imperial economy upon slave exploitation; or even by asserting that after the fall of Athens in 404 B.C. classical civilization was doomed.

Sometimes such explanations can absolutely be disproved. There is, for instance, no solid evidence of any change in climate or of exhaustion of the soil. Other factors can be shown to be merely attendant circumstances; malaria, thus, became more widespread as cultivation of the soil declined. More generalized explanations will commonly be found to have a close link with the social, religious, or intellectual preconceptions of the modern scholars who have advanced them; for in the end all students are really trying to explain the modern world when they speak of the past. And so, as their points of view may clash on the meaning of the present and hopes or fears of the future, so too vary their reconstructions of the past.

Phrase the Question of Rome's Fall in Wide Terms

Although this fact must at times disturb historical students who hope to find a certainty in history which they cannot establish in the present, it is not grounds for despair. The true test of historical spirit is the ability to broaden the preconceptions born of contemporary life as one investigates the complicated tissue of men's past development; for thereby one comes to understand more clearly not only the history of a past age but also the character of the world which surrounds us today. The student of the Roman Empire, thus, must always keep in mind that its history was not a simple one. On the one hand classical civilization became sterile, and the political and economic organization of the western provinces underwent a serious change which, as measured by earlier standards, must be called a decline. Yet at the same time a new scheme of thought about the most fundamental qualities of man was rising. Both developments, moreover, were long protracted in chains which extended back clearly to the second century after Christ and, less obviously, into earlier centuries.

Any explanation of the "decline and fall" must accordingly be phrased in wide terms; and it is the conviction of the present writer . . . that the historian must always come back to the movement of human emotion and the human mind in his deepest probings of the forces moving man's history. In this area one great key may be suggested which will perhaps unlock an understanding of the basic pattern—though not of all the ramifications—of the progress of imperial civilization. Mankind, that is to say, was liberated from its ties to state and to society in the Empire to a degree never before known, for the bonds of family and other social units, as well as active participation in political life, sharply diminished. One result [was] . . . the inability of men to create new thoughts within the inherited classical pattern. Another was their turn . . . to a new social and intellectual framework in Christianity, which bound them to each other and to a transcendental force above. To couple the old and new, however, was more than could be achieved once the political and economic structure of the western provinces had started to deteriorate . . . and those external pressures . . . accelerated the plunge. The full triumphs of the new outlook could not be achieved until western society had fashioned a new political and economic organization in the Middle Ages.

The Unity of Western Civilization

The long-range effects of the Germanic invasion and of the end of the Roman Empire in the west, to return to a remark made earlier, were perhaps not bad but rather essentially good. Politically, for instance, the result was to wipe out the despotism of the Later Empire. This despotism was really a "dead end" to ancient political development; for in it all political capacity had been concentrated in one man, aided by a corrupt, tyrannical bureaucracy which governed the subjects like cogs. The organization of the Germanic kingdoms was very simple, but it could proceed afresh on new lines; and not all that was useful in the past was lost. Regional ties in the Middle Ages could never quite wipe out the memory of the union of large areas under a single ruler. The kings of the western states became very weak, but they did not vanish; about these royal houses the modern national kingdoms were to rise. Beside the kings stood the Church, which preserved much of the administrative achievement and law of the Empire; but here too a basic principle of the ancient world, the union of Church and state, had essentially been broken.

Intellectually the view of man, of the world, and of God which underlay Christian thought was of a new order, which had broken through the limitations of ancient culture. When western Europe began to revive, its thinkers were able to drive forward on new lines, fructified [made productive] but not unduly hampered by the inheritance of the past; throughout the cultural diversity of medieval and modern times there lurks a concept of the unity of western civilization, based as it is—whether in Russia or in Britain—on a common classical background.

Economically, too, as one views the technological and social basis of ancient industry and commerce, one cannot see any possibility that this structure could have continued to expand indefinitely, or that it could have endured as political conditions worsened. The agricultural units which survived, the manors, resembled in many ways the villages from which urban life had sprung millennia before; yet the practice of agriculture in the Middle Ages was far above that of prehistoric times in variety and rotation of crops, quality of implements, and other important aspects, and the life of the nobles was, despite its rudeness, a thing unknown in the prehistoric era. One must also note that slavery virtually disappeared in western Europe; once the battle for survival had been won, the economic development of this area proceeded apace, and men might eventually hope to create a society in which not the few but the many could escape grinding poverty. An important factor in this possibility was the willingness of men in the medieval period to experiment and develop technology; new ways of doing things and of using nonhuman power—wind and water first—are a hallmark of the economic development of western Europe from the Middle Ages down to the present.

In sum the outward decay of the west was a necessary, if immediately devastating, step in its later surge; for in that decay the limiting bonds of ancient civilization were snapped. The other civilized areas of Eurasia clung more fully to their earlier cultures, and accordingly were the centers of intellectual and political life during the medieval period of western Europe. Yet once the energies of this relatively tiny area were unleashed, its peoples were to spring forward; the history of modern times is largely of the impact of that spring on the rest of the globe.

Appendix of Documents

Document 1: A Roman Predicts that All Nations Will Eventually Fall

In the first century A.D., *the brilliant Roman philosopher and scholar Seneca made this statement about the impermanence of all human societies. At the time, he was not necessarily predicting the fall of his own nation, which was still centuries in the future; but posterity ultimately proved him right, for even a realm as huge and powerful as the Roman Empire was not immune to the ravages of time, circumstance, and decay. And Seneca's words still stand as a warning to all peoples in all times.*

The entire human race, both present and future, is condemned to death. All the cities that have ever held dominion or have been the splendid jewels of empires belonging to others—some day men will ask where they were. And they will be swept away by various kinds of destruction: some will be ruined by wars, others will be destroyed by idleness and a peace that ends in sloth, or by luxury, the bane of those of great wealth. All these fertile plains will be blotted out of sight by a sudden overflowing of the sea, or the subsiding of the land will sweep them away suddenly into the abyss.

Seneca, *Moral Epistles 71.15.*

Document 2: The Germans Massacre a Roman Army

In A.D. *9, an army led by one of Augustus's officials was wiped out in the Teutoberg Forest in Germany. Though this event occurred when the Roman Empire was still young and strong, it underscored for the emperor and his subjects the danger posed by the so-called northern "barbarians" and was instrumental in changing Roman policy in that region. The disaster also foreshadowed the larger-scale barbarian encounters of later centuries. This description of the event is from the Roman history of the second-century Greek historian Dio Cassius.*

What had been happening in Germany during this period was as follows. The Romans had a hold on parts of it, not whole regions, but merely those areas which happened to have been subdued, so that this fact has not received historical notice. Meanwhile bodies of troops were in the habit of wintering there, and cities were being founded; the barbarians were gradually re-shaping their habits in conformity with the Roman pattern, were becoming accustomed to hold markets and were meeting in peaceful assemblies. But they had not forgotten their ancestral customs, their native manners, their independent way of life, nor the power they had enjoyed through their strength in arms. So long as they were unlearning their customs little by little, by indirect means, so to speak, and were under careful surveillance, they did not object to the change in their manner of life, and were unconsciously altering their disposition.

But when Quintilius Varus became governor of the province of Germany, and in the exercise of his powers also came to handle the affairs of these peoples, he tried both to hasten and to widen the process of change. He not only gave orders to the Germans as if they were actual slaves of the Romans, but also levied money from them as if they were subject nations. These were demands they would not tolerate. The leaders yearned for their former ascendancy, and the masses preferred their accustomed condition to foreign domination. They did not rise in open rebellion, because they saw that there were many Roman troops near the Rhine and many within their own territory. Instead, they received Varus, and by pretending that they would comply with all his orders, they lured him far away from the Rhine into the territory of the Cherusci and towards the river Visurgis. There they behaved in a most peaceful and friendly manner, and made him feel confident that they could live in a state of subjection without the presence of soldiers.

The result was that he did not keep his forces concentrated as was advisable in a hostile country, but dispersed many of his troops to those regions which lacked protection, supposedly to guard various vital positions, arrest outlaws or escort supply columns. . . .

And so the plan unfolded. The leaders escorted him as he set out, and then made their excuses for absenting themselves. This was to enable them, as they made out, to prepare their combined forces, after which they would quickly reassemble to support him. Then they took command of their troops which were already awaiting them in readiness somewhere. Next, after each community had slaughtered the detachments of Roman soldiers quartered with them, for which they had previously asked, they fell upon Varus in the midst of the forests, which at this point in his march were almost impenetrable. There, when they stood revealed as enemies instead of subjects, they dealt a succession of terrible blows to the Romans. . . .

The barbarians suddenly surrounded them on all sides at once, stealing through the densest thickets, as they were familiar with the paths. At first they hurled their spears from a distance, but as nobody attacked them in return and many were wounded, the Germans closed in to shorter range; for their part the Roman troops were not advancing in any regular formation, but were interspersed at random with the waggons and the non-combatants. This meant that they could not easily concentrate their strength at any point, and since they were everywhere overwhelmed by their opponents, they suffered many casualties and were quite unable to counter-attack.

Accordingly they pitched camp on the spot after taking possession of a suitable place, so far as one could be found on wooded and mountainous ground; afterwards they either burned or abandoned most of their waggons and everything else that was not absolutely indispensable to them. The next day they marched on in somewhat better order and even broke out into open country, though they could not avoid suffering casualties. Moving on from there they re-entered the woods, where they fought back against their assailants, but suffered their heaviest losses in this action. To enable the cavalry and infantry to make a combined charge against the enemy they had to form up in a narrow space, and so frequently collided with one another and with the trees. The fourth day saw them still on the move, and . . . they experienced heavy rain and violent winds, which prevented them from advancing or even finding a firm foothold and made it impossible to wield their weapons. They could neither draw their bows nor hurl their javelins to any effect, nor even make use of their shields, which were completely sodden with rain. Their opponents, on the other hand, were for the most part lightly armed, and so could approach or retire without difficulty, and suffered far less from the weather.

Besides this the enemy's numbers had been greatly reinforced, since many of those who had at first hesitated now joined the battle in the hope of taking plunder. Their increased numbers made it easier to encircle and strike down the Romans, whose ranks by contrast had shrunk, since they had lost many men in the earlier fighting. And so Varus and all the senior officers, fearing that they would either be taken alive or slaughtered by their bitterest enemies—for they had already been wounded—nerved themselves for the dreaded but unavoidable act, and took their own lives.

When this news spread to their men, none of the rest, even if strength remained, resisted any longer. Some followed the example of their general, others threw down their arms and allowed any who chose to slaughter them, since flight was out of the question, however much a man might desire it. So every soldier and every horse was cut down without resistance. . . .

At the time when Augustus learned of the disaster which had befallen Varus, he rent his clothes, according to some reports, and was overcome with grief. His feelings were not only of sorrow for the soldiers who had perished, but of fear for the provinces of Germany and of Gaul, above all because he expected that the enemy would invade Italy and even attack Rome itself. . . . At this time there were many Gauls and Germans actually living in Rome, some serving in the Praetorian Guard, and others residing there for various reasons. Augustus feared that these might start an uprising, and so despatched those who were serving in his bodyguard to various islands, and ordered those who were unarmed to leave the capital.

Dio Cassius, *The Roman History* 56. 18–22.

Document 3: A Roman Historian's View of the Germans

In his Germania, *the first-century* A.D. *Roman historian Tacitus provides this glimpse of life among the northern Germans, who would only a few centuries later overrun the western Empire. This excerpt describes their physical appearance, weapons, and leaders.*

For myself I accept the view that the peoples of Germany have never been tainted by intermarriage with other peoples, and stand out as a nation peculiar, pure and unique of its kind. Hence the physical type, if one may generalize at all about so vast a population, is everywhere the same—wild, blue eyes, reddish hair and huge frames that excel only in violent effort. They have no corresponding power to endure hard work and exertion, and have little capacity to bear thirst and heat; but their climate and soil *have* taught them to bear cold and hunger. . . .

Heaven has denied them gold and silver—shall I say in mercy or in wrath? But I would not go so far as to assert that Germany has no lodes of silver and gold. Who has ever prospected for them? The Germans take less than the normal pleasure in owning and using them. One may see among them silver vessels, which have been given as presents to their envoys and chiefs, as lightly esteemed as earthenware. The Germans nearest us do, however, value gold and silver for their use in trade, and recognize and prefer certain types of Roman money. The peoples of the interior, truer to the plain old ways, employ barter. . . .

There is not even any great abundance of iron [in Germany], as may be inferred from the character of their weapons. Only a very few use swords or lances. The spears that they carry—*frameae* is the native word—have short and narrow heads, but are so sharp and easy to handle, that the same weapon serves at need for close or distant fighting. The horseman asks no more than his shield and spear, but the infantry have also javelins to shower, several per man, and can hurl them to a great distance; for they are either naked or only lightly clad in their cloaks. There is nothing ostentatious in their turn-out. Only the shields are picked out with carefully selected colours. Few have breastplates; only here and there will you see a helmet of metal or hide. . . .

They choose their kings for their noble birth, their leaders for their valour. The power even of the kings is not absolute or arbitrary. As for the leaders, it is their example rather than their authority that wins them special admiration—for their energy, their distinction, or their presence in the van [front ranks] of fight. . . . They also carry into the fray figures and emblems taken from their sacred groves. Not chance or the accident of mustering makes the troop or wedge, but family and friendship, and this is a very powerful incitement to valour. A man's dearest possessions are at hand; he can hear close to him the laments of his women and the wailing of his children. These are the witnesses that a man reverences most, to them he looks for his highest praise. The men take their wounds to their mothers and wives, and the latter are not afraid of counting and examining the blows, and bring food and encouragement to the fighting men.

Tacitus, *Germania* 4–7.

Document 4: The Threat of Brigands in the Third Century

Among the many troubles endured by the inhabitants of the Empire in the crisis-ridden third century was the spread of large bands of brigands. In this excerpt from his history of Rome, Dio Cassius describes the difficulty the government had in capturing one such group.

At this period one Bulla, an Italian, got together a robber band of about six hundred men, and for two years continued to plunder Italy under the very noses of the emperors and of a multitude of soldiers. For though he was pursued by many men, and though [the emperor Septimius] Severus eagerly followed his trail, he was never really seen when seen, never found when found, never caught when caught, thanks to his great bribes and his cleverness. For he learned about everybody that was setting out from Rome and everybody that was putting into port at Brundisium, and knew both who and how many there were, and what and how much they had with them. In the case of most persons he would take a part of what they had and let them go at once, but he detained artisans for a time and made use of their skill, then dismissed them with a present. Once when two of his robber band had been captured and were about to be given to wild beasts, he paid a visit to the prison keeper, pretending that he was a magistrate of his native district and needed some men of this kind, and in this way he secured and saved the men. And he approached the centurion who was trying to exterminate the band and accused himself, pretending to be someone else, and promised, if the centurion would accompany him, to deliver the robber to him. So, on the pretext that he was leading him to Felix (this was another name by which he was called), he led him into a defile beset with thickets, and easily seized him. Later, he assumed the dress of a magistrate, ascended the tribunal, and having summoned the centurion caused part of his head to be shaved, and then said, "Carry this message to your masters: 'Feed your slaves, so that they may not turn to brigandage.'" Bulla had with him, in fact, a very large number of imperial freedmen, some of whom had been poorly paid, while others had received absolutely no pay at all.

Dio Cassius, *The Roman History* 76.10.1–5.

Document 5: Civil Strife Destroys a Prosperous City

Probably of Syrian birth, the Greek writer Herodian, who died about A.D. 238–240, penned a history of the Roman world covering events of the late second and early third centuries. This excerpt vividly captures the wanton destruction of the town of Aquileia, near the northern coast of the Adriatic Sea, by the army of the emperor Maximinus. This was only one of many cities that met such a fate during the period known as the "Anarchy."

Aquileia was even in earlier times a very big city with a large population of its own. Situated on the sea like an emporium of Italy and fronting all the Illyrian peoples, she provided the merchants sailing there with the products received from the interior by land or river, and she shipped into the hinterland the products from overseas needed by the inhabitants, which their land did not readily produce because of its cold climate; and also, as they did not cultivate the vine and her territory was especially productive of wine, she furnished them with an abundance of drink. Accordingly, a large population lived there, consisting not only of citizens but also of foreigners and merchants. At this time [A.D. 238] however, the population was even further increased by all the crowds streaming thither from the countryside, leaving the neighboring towns and villages to seek safety inside the great city and its surrounding wall. The ancient wall had for the most part been demolished earlier, since after the advent of Roman rule the cities of Italy no longer needed walls or weapons, for they enjoyed, in place of wars, profound peace and association in Roman citizenship. But now necessity drove them to restore the wall, rebuild its ruins, and raise towers and battlements. . . .

When he came to a very big river sixteen miles distant from the city, Maximinus found the stream at its greatest depth and width. . . . There was no way for the army to cross, for the Aquileians had torn down and destroyed the bridge. . . . Setting up [a pontoon bridge laid on large wine casks], the army crossed over and marched upon the city. Finding the houses of the suburbs deserted, they cut down all the vines and trees, set some on fire, and made a shambles of the once-thriving countryside. . . . After destroying all this to the root, the army pressed on to the walls . . . and strove to demolish at least some part of the wall, so that they might break in and sack everything, razing the city and leaving the land a deserted pasturage.

Herodian, *History of the Empire After Marcus* 8.2–4.

Document 6: The Consequences of Barbarization

Some Roman emperors settled barbarian tribes on Roman soil and enlisted barbarian warriors in the Roman army. This description of the negative consequences of this policy in the case of the emperor Probus (reigned 276–282) is by an unknown fourth-century writer whose biographies of Roman leaders were later collected as the Augustan History.

He took 16,000 [German] recruits, all of whom he scattered through the various provinces, incorporating bodies of fifty or sixty in the detachments or among the soldiers along the frontier, for he said that the aid that the Romans received from barbarian auxiliaries must be felt but not seen. . . . Having made peace, then, with the Persians, he returned to Thrace, where he settled 100,000 Bastarnians on Roman soil, all of whom remained loyal. But when he had likewise brought over many from other tribes—that is, Gepedians, Greuthungians, and Vandals—they all broke faith, and when Probus was busied with wars against the pretenders they roamed over well-nigh the entire world on foot or in ships and did no little damage to the glory of Rome.

Augustan History, Life of Probus 14.7, 18.1–2.

Document 7: The Problem of Military Discipline

The breakdown of military discipline in the third-century crisis was so severe that army leaders eventually had to resort to harsh penalties to reinforce it. This tract from Augustan History *describes the no-nonsense rules of the soldier-emperor Aurelian (reigned 270–275).*

Aurelian was so feared by the soldiers that, under him, after offenses had once been punished by him in the camp with the utmost severity, no one offended again. . . . There is a letter of his, truly that of a soldier, written to his deputy as follows: "If you wish to be a tribune, or rather if you wish to remain alive, restrain the hands of your soldiers. None shall steal another's fowl or touch his sheep. None shall carry off grapes, or thresh out grain, or exact oil, salt, or firewood, and each shall be content with his own allowance. Let them have these things from the booty taken from the enemy and not from the tears of the provincials. Their arms shall be kept burnished, their implements bright, their boots stout. Let old uniforms be replaced by new. Let them keep their pay in their belts and not spend it in public houses. Let them wear their collars, arm rings, and finger rings. Let each man curry his own horse and baggage animal, let no one sell the fodder allowed him for his beast, and let them take care in common of the mule belonging to the century. Let one yield obedience to another as to a master, and no one as a slave, let them be attended by physicians without charge, let them give no fees to soothsayers, let them conduct themselves in their lodgings with propriety, and let anyone who begins a brawl be thrashed."

Augustan History, Life of Aurelian 7.

Document 8: Diocletian Attempts to Set Maximum Prices

Following are excerpts from Diocletian's famous Economic Edict *issued in 301, in which he attempted (ultimately in vain) to stabilize the Roman economy by setting maximum prices that people could charge for goods and services.*

We, who by the gracious favor of the gods have repressed the former tide of ravages of barbarian nations by destroying them, must guard by the due defenses of justice a peace which was established for eternity. If, indeed, any self-restraint might check the excesses with which limitless and furious avarice [greed] rages . . . there would perhaps be some room for . . . silence [inaction]. . . . Since, however, it is the sole desire of unrestrained madness to have no thought for the common need . . . we—the protectors of the human race—viewing the situation, have agreed that justice should intervene . . . so that the long-hoped-for solution which mankind itself could not supply might . . . be applied to the general betterment of all. . . . We, therefore, hasten to apply the remedies long demanded by the situation, satisfied that there can be no complaints. . . . For who is so insensitive and devoid of human feeling that he cannot know . . . that in the commerce carried on in the markets . . . immoderate prices are so widespread. . . . Aroused justly and rightfully by all the facts which are detailed above, and with mankind itself now appearing to be praying for release [from economic misery], we have decreed that there be established . . . a maximum [ceiling for prices and wages], so that when the violence of high prices appears anywhere—may the gods avert such a calamity! . . . It is our pleasure, therefore, that the prices listed in the subjoined [attached] summary be observed in the whole of our empire. . . . We . . . urge upon the loyalty of all our people that a law constituted for the public good may be observed with willing obedience and due care.

Diocletian's *Edict on Prices*, in *Corpus Inscriptionum Latinarum*, vol. 3.

Document 9: Diocletian and Galerius Persecute the Christians

In this tract from his work, The Deaths of the Persecutors, *the Christian writer Lactantius describes the beginning of the terrible persecution against the Christian sect ordered in 303 by the emperor Diocletian and his Caesar (subordinate co-emperor), Galerius.*

Suddenly, while it was still not full daylight, the prefect came to the church with leaders and tribunes and officers of the treasury. They tore down the door and searched for a picture or image of God. When the Scriptures were found, they were burned. The chance for booty was given to all. There was pillaging, trepidation, running about all around. . . .

The next day the edict was published in which it was ordered that men of that religion should be deprived of all honor and dignity and be subjected to torments; and no matter from what rank or grade they came every action against them would hold weight; and they themselves would not be able to plead in a court against a charge of injury or adultery or theft; in short, they would not have freedom of speech. Although it was not right, still it was with great courage that a certain man pulled down and tore up this edict, as he said deridingly that victories of the Goths and Sarmatians were proposed in it. Immediately, he was taken, and he was not only tortured, but he was actually cooked, according to the directions of a particular recipe, and then finally burned up, having suffered with admirable patience.

But the Caesar was not content with the laws of the edict. He prepared to set Diocletian off on another score. In order to drive him to the determination of the most cruel persecution, he set fire to the palace through the aid of secret agents. And when part had been burned, the Christians were charged with being public enemies and, because ill-will was so high, the name of the Christians was being burned along with the palace.

Lactantius, *The Deaths of the Persecutors* 7–14.

Document 10: A Roman Christian Pleads for Fair Treatment

Tertullian was the first great Latin Christian writer. This excerpt from his Apology *was written in 197 B.C., well before Diocletian's persecution; however, it reflected the same appeal made by early fourth-century Christians to all fair-minded Romans, pleading with them to stop the negative stereotyping and abuse of the Christians. The emperor Constantine, of course, soon heard and sympathized with this appeal.*

Magistrates of the Roman Empire, seated as you are before the eyes of all, in almost the highest position in the state to pronounce judgment: if you are not to conduct an open and public examination and inquiry as to what the real truth is with regard to the Christians; if, in this case alone your authority fears or blushes to conduct a public investigation with the diligence demanded by justice; if, in fine—as happened lately in the private courts—hatred of this group has been aroused to the extent that it actually blocks their defense, then let the truth reach your ears by the private and quiet avenue of literature. . . .

This, then, is the first grievance we lodge against you, the injustice of the hatred you have for the name of Christian. The motive which appears to excuse this injustice is precisely that which both aggravates and convicts it; namely, ignorance. For, what is more unjust than that men should hate what they do not know, even though the matter itself deserves hatred? Only when one knows whether a thing deserves hatred does it deserve it. But, when there is no knowledge of what is deserved, how is the justice of hatred defensible? Justice must be proved not by the fact of a thing's existence, but by knowledge of it. When men hate because they are in ignorance of the nature of the object of their hatred, what is to prevent that object from being such that they ought not to hate it? Thus we counterbalance each attitude by its opposite: men remain in ignorance as long as they hate, and they hate unjustly as long as they remain in ignorance. . . .

If, then, it is decided that we are the most wicked of men, why do you treat us so differently from those who are on a par with us, that is, from all other criminals? The same treatment ought to be meted out for the same crime. When others are charged with the same crimes as we, they use their own lips and the hired eloquence of others to prove their innocence. There is full liberty given to answer the charge and to cross-question, since it is unlawful for men to be condemned without defense or without a hearing. Christians alone are permitted to say nothing that would clear their name, vindicate the truth, and aid the judge to come to a fair decision. One thing only is what they wait for; this is the only thing necessary to arouse public hatred: the confession of the name of Christian, not an investigation of the charge. Yet, suppose you are trying any other criminal. If he confesses to the crime of murder, sacrilege, incest, or treason—to particularize the indictments hurled against us—you are not satisfied to pass sentence immediately; you weigh the attendant circumstances, the character of the deed, the number of times it was committed, the time, the place, the witnesses, and the partners-in-crime. In our case there is nothing of this sort. No matter what false charge is made against us, we must be made to confess it.

Tertullian, *Apology* 1.

Document 11: The Christians Granted Religious Freedom

In his Ecclesiastical History, *the fourth-century Christian writer Eusebius recorded the famous* Edict of Milan, *parts of which are presented here. In the document, made public in 313, the emperors Constantine and Licinius granted religious freedom to the Christians.*

When under happy auspices I, Constantine Augustus, and I, Licinius Augustus, had come to Milan and held an inquiry about all matters such as pertain to the common advantage and good, these things along with the others that seemed to benefit the many, or rather, first and foremost, we resolved to issue decrees by which esteem and reverence for the Deity might be procured, that is, that we might give all Christians freedom of choice to follow the ritual which they wished, so that whatever is of the nature of the divine and heavenly might be propitious to us and to all those living under our authority. Accordingly, with sound and most correct reasoning we decided upon this our plan: that authority is to be refused no one at all to follow and to choose the observance or the form of worship of the Christians, and that authority be given to each one to devote his mind to that form of worship which he himself considers to be adapted to himself, in order that the Deity may be able in all things to provide for us His accustomed care and goodness. . . .

And since the same Christians had not only those places in which they used to assemble, but are known to have had others, also, which belonged not to individuals among them, but to the rightful claim of their whole body, that is, of the Christians, all these, in accordance with the law which we have just mentioned, you are to order to be restored without delay to the same Christians, that is, to their group and to each assembly, guarding clearly the aforementioned statement, that whoever restore the same places without compensation, even as we have already said, may hope for indemnification from our own generosity.

In all these matters you should exercise the utmost care for the aforementioned group of Christians, so that our order may be carried out as quickly as possible, and that also in this forethought may be exercised through our beneficence for the common and public peace. For by this means, as has been mentioned before, the divine zeal in our behalf, which we have already experienced in many things, will remain steadfast forever. And that the scope of this our decree and generosity may be brought to the knowledge of all, it is fitting that these matters as decreed by us be declared everywhere, and brought to the knowledge of all by being published at your order, so that the decree of this our generosity may escape the notice of no one.

Edict of Milan in Eusebius, *Ecclesiastical History* 10.5.3–14.

Document 12: Constantine Reorganizes the Empire

Zosimus was a fifth-century Greek historian whose major work covered the period from Diocletian's reign (in the late third century) to Alaric's sacking of Rome (in 410). In this excerpt, Zosimus tells about Constantine's increase in the number of Praetorian prefects (whose troops guarded

the city of Rome) and then criticizes the emperor for weakening the fron-
tier military garrisons. Many modern historians agree with Zosimus's
assessment that the latter move seriously weakened the Empire in the
long run.

Constantine drastically reorganized the long-established offices.
There had been two Praetorian prefects, who administered the office jointly and controlled by their supervision and power not only
the Praetorian cohorts but also those which were entrusted with
the guarding of the city and those which were stationed in the out-
skirts. The office of Praetorian prefect had been considered second to that of the emperor; he made the distributions of grain and
redressed all offenses against military discipline by appropriate
punishments. Constantine, altering this good institution, divided
the single office into four. . . .

   Constantine likewise took another measure, which gave the
barbarians unhindered access into the lands subject to the Romans.
For the Roman Empire was, by the foresight of Diocletian, everywhere protected on its frontiers . . . by towns and fortresses and
towers, in which the entire army was stationed; it was thus impossible for the barbarians to cross over, there being everywhere a sufficient opposing force to repel their inroads. But Constantine destroyed that security by removing the greater part of the soldiers
from the frontiers and stationing them in cities that did not require
protection; thus he stripped those of protection who were harassed
by the barbarians and brought ruin to peaceful cities at the hands
of the soldiers, with the result that most have become deserted. He
likewise softened the soldiers by exposing them to shows and lux-
uries. To speak plainly, he was the first to sow the seeds of the ru-
inous state of affairs that has lasted up to the present time.

Zosimus, *Recent History* 2.32–35.

Document 13: Ammianus Lists the Vices of the Roman Nobles

Ammianus Marcellinus was the greatest Latin historian of the Later
Empire. In this excerpt from the surviving books of his great history, he
paints an unflattering portrait of a morally declining nobility, many
members of which, he claims, have degenerated into arrogant, insensi-
tive, and hypocritical boors.

I will deal first with the faults of the nobility. . . . Some plume
themselves on what they consider distinguished forenames, such
as Reburrus, Flavonius, Pagonius, and Gereon, or trace their de-

scent from the Dalii or Tarracii or Ferasii or some other high-sounding family. Some, dressed in gleaming silk, go about preceded by a crowd of people, like men being led to execution or, to avoid so unfortunate a simile, like men bringing up the rear of an army, and are followed by a throng of noisy slaves in formation. When such people, each attended by a train of some fifty, enter the public baths, they shout in a peremptory voice: "What has become of our girls?". . .

If one tries to greet these people with an embrace they turn their head to one side like a bad-tempered bull, though that is the natural place for a kiss, and offer their knee or their hand instead, as if that should be enough to make anyone happy for life. . . .

Their houses are the resort of idle gossips, who greet every word uttered by the great man with various expressions of hypocritical applause, like the toady in the comedy who inflates the pride of the boastful soldier by attributing to him heroic exploits in sieges and in fights against overwhelming odds. . . .

A few of them treat offenses with such severity that a slave who is slow in bringing hot water will be ordered 300 lashes. But if he should have deliberately killed someone and there is a general demand for his punishment, his master will merely exclaim: "What else can you expect of such a worthless rascal? If he does anything like this again he shall pay for it.". . .

Some of these people, though not many, dislike the name of gamblers and prefer to be called dice-players, though the distinction is no more than that between a thief and a robber. It must be admitted, however, that, while all other friendships at Rome are lukewarm, those between gamblers are as close and are maintained with as much steadfast affection as if they had been forged by common effort in a glorious cause.

Ammianus Marcellinus, *History* 28.4.6–21.

Document 14: The Military Catastrophe at Adrianople

Following is a major portion of Ammianus's moving account of the disastrous battle of Adrianople, fought in 378 in Thrace, in which as many as 40,000 Roman troops, along with their commander, the eastern emperor Valens, met their doom. After this crushing defeat at the hands of the Visigoths, Rome's military decline proceeded at an accelerating pace.

When dawn came on the day marked in the calendar as 9 August, the army was put in rapid motion. All its impedimenta and baggage were left near the walls of Adrianople under an adequate guard, and the praetorian prefect and members of the consistory remained inside the town with the treasure-chests and the imperial insignia. After a march of eight miles over rough country under a burning mid-day sun our troops came within sight of the enemy's waggons, which, as our scouts had reported, were drawn up in a regular circle. While the enemy in their usual way were raising a wild and doleful yell, the Roman generals marshalled their line of battle. The cavalry on the right wing were furthest advanced, and the greater part of the infantry were some way to their rear. But the cavalry of our left wing were still straggling along the road, making what speed they could but under serious difficulties. . . .

[Just when it appeared that a truce might be arranged] the archers and Scutarii [on the Roman side] commanded by Cassio and by the Iberian Bacurius impulsively launched a hot attack and engaged the enemy. Their retreat was as cowardly as their advance had been rash, a most inauspicious start to the battle. This untimely proceeding . . . brought on an attack by the Gothic cavalry under Alatheus and Saphrax, who had now arrived supported by a party of Alans. They shot forward *like a bolt from on high* and routed with great slaughter all that they could come to grips with in their wild career.

Amid the clashing of arms and weapons on every side, while Bellona [Roman goddess of war], raging with more than her usual fury, was sounding the death-knell of the Roman cause, our retreating troops rallied with shouts of mutual encouragement. But, as the fighting spread like fire and numbers of them were transfixed by arrows and whirling javelins, they lost heart. Then the opposing lines came into collision like ships of war and pushed each other to and fro, heaving under the reciprocal motion like the waves of the sea. Our left wing penetrated as far as the very waggons, and would have gone further if it had received any support, but it was abandoned by the rest of the cavalry, and under pressure of numbers gave way and collapsed like a broken dyke. This left the infantry unprotected and so closely huddled together that a man could hardly wield his sword or draw back his arm once he had stretched it out. Dust rose in such clouds as to hide the sky, which rang with frightful shouts. In consequence it was impossible to see the enemy's missiles in flight and dodge them; all found their mark and dealt death on every side. The barbarians poured on in huge columns, trampling down horse and man and crushing our ranks so as to make an orderly retreat impossible. Our men were too close-packed to have any hope of escape; so they resolved to die like heroes, faced the enemy's swords, and struck back at their assailants. On both sides helmets and breast-plates were split in pieces by blows from the battle-axe. You might see a lion-hearted savage, who had been hamstrung or had lost his right hand or been wounded in the side, grinding his clenched teeth and casting defiant glances around in the very throes of death. In this mutual slaughter so many were laid low that the field was covered with the bodies of the slain, while the groans of the dying and severely wounded filled all who heard them with abject fear.

In this scene of total confusion the infantry, worn out by toil and danger, had no strength or sense left to form a plan. Most had had their spears shattered in the constant collisions, so they made do with their drawn swords and plunged into the dense masses of the foe, regardless of their lives and aware that there was no hope of escape. The ground was so drenched with blood that they slipped and fell, but they strained every nerve to sell their lives dearly, and faced their opponents with such resolution that some perished at the hands of their own comrades. In the end, when the whole field was one dark pool of blood and they could see nothing but heaps of slain wherever they turned their eyes, they trampled without scruple on the lifeless corpses.

The sun, which was high in the sky (it was moving into the house of the Virgin after traversing Leo), scorched the Romans, who were weak from hunger, parched with thirst, and weighed down by the burden of their armour. Finally, our line gave way under the overpowering pressure of the barbarians, and as a last resort our men took to their heels. . . .

The barbarians' eyes flashed fire as they pursued their dazed foe, whose blood ran cold with terror. Some fell without knowing who struck them, some were crushed by sheer weight of numbers, and some were killed by their own comrades. They could neither gain ground by resistance nor obtain mercy by giving way. Besides, many lay blocking the way half dead, unable to endure the agony of their wounds, and the carcasses of slaughtered horses covered the ground in heaps. At last a moonless night brought an end to these irreparable losses, which cost Rome so dear.

Soon after nightfall, so it was supposed, the emperor was mortally wounded by an arrow and died immediately. No one admitted that he had seen him or been near him, and it was presumed that he fell among common soldiers, but his body was never found. A few of the enemy were hanging about the field for some time to strip the dead, so that none of the fugitives or local people dared to approach. . . . According to another account, Valens did not expire on the spot, but was taken with a few of his guards and some eunuchs to a farmhouse nearby, which had a fortified second storey. While he was receiving such rude treatment as was available he was surrounded by the enemy, though they did not know who he was. But he was spared the shame of being taken prisoner. His pursuers tried to break down the doors, which were bolted, but came under arrow-fire from the overhanging part of the building. In order not to let this delay rob them of their chance of spoil, they piled up bundles of straw . . . set fire to them, and burned the house with all who were in it. One of the guards escaped through a window and was taken prisoner. He told them what they had done, which greatly vexed them, because they had lost the glory of taking the ruler of Rome alive. . . .

It is certain that hardly a third of our army escaped. *No battle* in our history except Cannae was such a massacre, though more than once the Romans have been the playthings of fortune and suffered temporary reverses, and many disastrous struggles are recorded with grief in the legendary sagas of Greece.

Ammianus Marcellinus, *History* 31.13.

Document 15: St. Jerome Laments the Sacking of Rome

In his now well-known letter number 127, extolling the virtues of a noble Roman woman named Marcella, the Christian writer Jerome, who lived from about 345 to 420, captured the feelings of shock and sadness that many of his countrymen must have felt on hearing the news of the sacking of Rome by the Visigoths in 410.

While these things were taking place in Jebus [Jerusalem], a dreadful rumour reached us from the West. We heard that Rome was besieged, that the citizens were buying their safety with gold, and that when they had been thus despoiled they were again beleaguered, so as to lose not only their substance but their lives. The speaker's voice failed and sobs interrupted his utterance. The city which had taken the whole world was itself taken; nay, it fell by famine before it fell by the sword, and there were but a few found to be made prisoners. The rage of hunger had recourse to impious food; men tore one another's limbs, and the mother did not spare the baby at her breast, taking again within her body that which her body had just brought forth. . . .

Who can tell that night of havoc, who can shed
    enough of tears

For those deaths? The ancient city that for many
    a hundred years
Ruled the world comes down in ruin: corpses lie in
    every street
And men's eyes in every household death in
    countless phases meet.

Jerome, *Letters 127.*

Document 16: Occupations Still Hereditary by Law in the Fifth Century

In 438, the government of emperor Theodosius II published a compila-tion of all laws enacted since 312, when Constantine was in power. This Theodosian Code *included a number of decrees dealing with the rules, and also the exceptions to the rules, that required people to practice the same occupations as their fathers, a policy originally designed to keep the flow of goods and services stable. The two brief examples that follow con-sist of laws originally created between 313 and 315.*

Of the veterans' sons who are fit for military service, some indo-lently object to the performance of their compulsory military du-ties and others are so cowardly that they desire to evade the ne-cessity of military service by mutilation of their bodies. If they should be judged useless for military service because of amputated fingers, we order them to be assigned to the compulsory services and duties of decurions with no ambiguity. . . .

Shipmasters nominated to the guild of city breadmakers but not subject to these breadmakers by any succession of inheritance must be released from this compulsory public service. But if they should chance to be bound to the breadmakers by hereditary right, they shall have the opportunity, if they perchance prefer, to relinquish the adventitious inheritance of breadmakers to the said guild or yield it to any next of kin of the deceased, in order to free themselves from the guild of breadmakers. But if they embrace the inheritance, it is necessary for them to undertake association in the compulsory public service of breadmaking by reason of the inheritance, and to sustain from their own resources the burdens of shipmasters.

Theodosian Code 22.1, 13.5.

Document 17: The Poor Burdened by Heavy Taxation

Salvian (or Salvianus), a Christian priest and writer who lived from about 400 to 480, left behind this strong denunciation of tax laws and collectors who victimized the poor during the last years of the western Empire. Salvian's claim that many poor Romans took refuge with the barbarians to escape Roman tax collectors is likely little exaggerated.

But what else can these wretched people wish for, they who suffer the incessant and even continuous destruction of public tax levies. To them there is always imminent a heavy and relentless proscription. They desert their homes, lest they be tortured in their very homes. They seek exile, lest they suffer torture. The enemy is more lenient to them than the tax collectors. This is proved by this very fact, that they flee to the enemy in order to avoid the full force of the heavy tax levy. This very tax levying, although hard and inhuman, would nevertheless be less heavy and harsh if all would bear it equally and in common. Taxation is made more shameful and burdensome because all do not bear the burden of all. They extort tribute from the poor man for the taxes of the rich, and the weaker carry the load for the stronger. There is no other reason that they cannot bear all the taxation except that the burden imposed on the wretched is greater than their resources. . . .

Do we think we are unworthy of the punishment of divine severity when we thus constantly punish the poor? Do we think, when we are constantly wicked, that God should not exercise His justice against all of us? Where or in whom are evils so great, except among the Romans? Whose injustice so great except our own? The Franks are ignorant of this crime of injustice. The Huns are immune to these crimes. There are no wrongs among the Vandals and none among the Goths. So far are the barbarians from tolerating these injustices among the Goths, that not even the Romans who live among them suffer them.

Therefore, in the districts taken over by the barbarians, there is one desire among all the Romans, that they should never again find it necessary to pass under Roman jurisdiction. In those regions, it is the one and general prayer of the Roman people that they be allowed to carry on the life they lead with the barbarians. And we wonder why the Goths are not conquered by our portion of the population, when the Romans prefer to live among them rather than with us. Our brothers, therefore, are not only altogether unwilling to flee to us from them, but they even cast us aside in order to flee to them.

Salvian, *On the Governance of God*, in *The Middle Ages, Volume I: Sources of Medieval History*.

Document 18: In Rome's Twilight, Praise for Its Justice and Glory

Rutilius Namatianus, born in the late fourth century, was the last of the classical Latin poets. This excerpt from his Voyage Home to Gaul, *composed in 416, is often called "Rome's Swan Song," because, in contrast to the gloomy picture of a decaying civilization painted by Salvian and other Christian writers of the period, Rutilius sings the praises of traditional Rome, which he sees as still majestic and eternal. This suggests that many Romans remained optimistic and could not conceive that their world was nearing its end.*

Listen, O fairest queen of thy world, Rome, welcomed amid the starry skies, listen, thou mother of men and mother of gods, thanks to thy temples we are not far from heaven: thee do we chant, and shall, while destiny allows, for ever chant. None can be safe if forgetful of thee. Sooner shall guilty oblivion [over]whelm the sun than the honour due to thee quit my heart: for thy benefits extend as far as the sun's rays, where the circling Ocean-flood bounds the world. For thee the very Sun-God who holdeth all together doth revolve: his steeds that rise in thy domains he puts in thy domains to rest. Thee Africa hath not stayed with scorching sands, nor hath the Bear, armed with its native cold, repulsed thee. As far as living nature hath stretched towards the poles, so far hath earth opened a path for thy valour. For nations far apart thou hast made a single fatherland; under thy dominion captivity hath meant profit even for those who knew not justice: and by offering to the vanquished a share in thine own justice, thou hast made a city of what was erstwhile a world. . . .

Spread forth the laws that are to last throughout the ages of Rome: alone thou needst not dread the distaffs of the Fates. . . . The span which doth remain is subject to no bounds, so long as earth shall stand firm and heaven uphold the stars!

Rutilius Namatianus, *Voyage Home to Gaul* 1.46–66, 133–138.

Document 19: Life in Fifth-Century Barbarian Gaul

Apollinaris Sidonius was a Roman country gentleman who lived in Gaul, what is now France, from about 430 to 487. When he wrote the fascinating letters excerpted below, circa 465–470, most of the old Roman aristocratic families of the region had for some time lived in comparative harmony with the "barbarians," who, as Sidonius illustrates, were much more civilized than this pejorative nickname suggests.

I have passed the most delightful time in the most beautiful country [southern France] in the company of Tonantius Ferreolus and Apollinaris, the most charming hosts in the world. Their estates march together; their houses are not far apart; and the extent of intervening ground is just too far for a walk and just too short to make the ride worth while. The hills above the houses are under vines and olives; . . . the view from one villa is over a wide flat country, that from the other over woodland; yet different though their situations are, the eye derives equal pleasure from both. But enough of sites; I have now to unfold the order of my entertainment. . . . From the first moment we were hurried from one pleasure to another. Hardly had we entered the vestibule of either house when we saw two opposed pairs of partners in the ball-game repeating each other's movements as they turned in wheeling circles; in another place one heard the rattle of dice boxes and the shouts of the contending players; in yet another, were books in abundance ready to your hand. . . .

You take such pleasure in the sight of arms and those who wear them, that I can imagine your delight if you could have seen the young prince Sigismer on his way to the palace of his father-in-law in the guise of a bridegroom or suitor in all the pomp and bravery of the tribal fashion. His own steed with its caparisons, other steeds laden with flashing gems, paced before and after; but the conspicuous interest in the procession centred in the prince himself, as with a charming modesty he went afoot amid his bodyguard and footmen, in flame-red mantle, with much glint of ruddy gold, and gleam of snowy silken tunic, his fair hair, red cheeks and white skin according with the three hues of his equipment. But the chiefs and allies who bore him company were dread of aspect, even thus on peace intent. Their feet were laced in boots of bristly hide reaching to the heels; ankles and legs were exposed. They wore high tight tunics of varied color hardly descending to their bare knees, the sleeves covering only the upper arm. Green mantles they had with crimson borders. . . . No small part of their adornment consisted of their arms; in their hands they grasped barbed spears and missile axes; their left sides were guarded by shields, which flashed with tawny golden bosses and snowy silver borders, betraying at once their wealth and their good taste.

Sidonius, *Letters* 7.

Document 20: Theodoric: An Enlightened "Barbarian" Ruler

Theodoric the Ostrogoth ruled Italy as its king from 493 to 526, having pushed aside Odoacer, who himself had deposed the last western Roman emperor. These brief excerpts from two letters drafted by Theodoric's secretary, the Roman statesman and historian Cassiodorus (ca. 490–585), reveal that this king, a so-called barbarian, was a more enlightened and caring ruler than most of the emperors of the Later Empire. The first letter addresses the Senate, which by this time held no real power, with great respect; the other appeals to a barbarian chief to live according to Roman law.

King Theodoric to the Senate of the City of Rome
We hear with sorrow, by the report of the Provincial Judges, that you the Fathers of the State, who ought to set an example to your sons (the ordinary citizens), have been so remiss in the payment of taxes that on this first collection nothing, or next to nothing, has been brought in from any Senatorial house. Thus a crushing weight has fallen on the lower orders, who have had to make good your deficiencies and have been distraught by the violence of the tax-gatherers.

Now then, oh Conscript Fathers, who owe as much duty to the Republic as we do, pay the taxes for which each one of you is liable, to the Procurators appointed in each Province, by three instalments. Or, if you prefer to do so—and it used to be accounted a privilege—pay all at once into the chest of the Vicarious. And let this following edict be published, that all the Provincials may know that they are not to be imposed upon and that they are invited to state their grievances.

King Theodoric to Unigis, the Sword-Bearer
We delight to live after the law of the Romans, whom we seek to defend with our arms; and we are as much interested in the maintenance of morality as we can possibly be in war. For what profit is there in having removed the turmoil of the Barbarians, unless we live according to law? . . . Let other kings desire the glory of battles won, of cities taken, of ruins made; our purpose is, God helping us, so to rule that our subjects shall grieve that they did not earlier acquire the blessing of our dominion.

Cassiodorus, quoted in *The Middle Ages, Volume I: Sources of Medieval History.*

Chronology

753
Traditional founding date for the city-state of Rome.

509
The leading Roman landowners throw out their last king and establish the Roman Republic.

44
After declaring himself dictator, politician and military general Julius Caesar is assassinated by a group of disgruntled senators, pushing the Roman world, already exhausted from a recent series of destructive civil wars, toward more chaos and bloodshed.

31
In the Republic's final power struggle, Caesar's adopted son, Octavian, defeats his last rivals at Actium (in western Greece) and gains firm control of the Mediterranean world.

27
With the blessings of the Senate, Octavian takes the name of Augustus. Historians usually mark this date as the beginning of the Roman Empire, with Augustus as its first emperor (although he himself never used that title, preferring to call himself "first citizen").

ca. 30 B.C.–A.D. 180
Approximate years of the so-called *Pax Romana*, a period in which the Mediterranean world under the first several Roman emperors enjoys relative peace and prosperity.

A.D.

98–117
Reign of the emperor Trajan, in which the Roman Empire reaches its greatest size and power.

180
Death of the emperor Marcus Aurelius, marking the end of the *Pax Romana* era and beginning of Rome's steady slide into economic and political crisis.

193–235

Period of the combined reigns of the emperors of the Severan dynasty, beginning with Septimius Severus and ending with Alexander Severus.

212

Caracalla, Septimius Severus's son, extends citizenship rights to all free adult males in the Empire.

235–284

The Empire nearly collapses under the strain of terrible political anarchy and civil strife.

284

Military man Diocletian becomes emperor and initiates sweeping political, economic, social, and military reforms, in effect reconstructing the Empire under a new blueprint.

293

Diocletian establishes the first "Tetrarchy," a power-sharing arrangement in which two emperors (with the title of Augustus) reign, one in the East, the other in the West, each with an assistant (with the title of Caesar).

307–337

Reign of the emperor Constantine I, who carries on the reforms begun by Diocletian.

312

Constantine defeats his rival, the usurper Maxentius, at Rome's Milvian Bridge. Constantine credits the Christian god for his victory.

313

Constantine and his eastern colleague, Licinius, issue the so-called Edict of Milan, granting religious toleration to the formerly hated and persecuted Christian sect.

330

Constantine founds the city of Constantinople, on the Bosphorus Strait, making it the capital of the eastern section of the Empire.

361–363

Reign of the emperor Julian, a brilliant and capable individual who, in the face of Christianity's growing popularity, tries but fails to reestablish paganism as Rome's dominant religion.

375

The Huns, a savage nomadic people from central Asia, sweep into eastern Europe, pushing the Goths and other "barbarian" peoples into Rome's northern provinces.

378

The eastern emperor Valens is disastrously defeated by the Visigoths at Adrianople (in the Greek region of Thrace).

395

The emperor Theodosius I, the Great, dies, leaving his sons Arcadius and Honorius in control of a permanently divided Roman Empire.

ca. 407

As Rome steadily loses control of several of its northern and western provinces, Britain falls under the sway of barbarian tribes.

410

The Visigoths, led by their war chief, Alaric, sack Rome.

418

The Visigoths invade Gaul, encountering little resistance.

455

Rome is sacked again, this time by the Vandals, led by Gaiseric.

476

The German-born general Odoacer (or Odovacar) demands that the western Roman government grant him and his men federate status and Italian lands; when the demand is refused, he deposes the young emperor Romulus Augustulus. Later historians came to see this event as the "fall" of Rome, although Roman life went on more or less as usual for some time under Odoacer and other Germanic rulers.

493

Theodoric the Ostrogoth seizes power from Odoacer.

527–565

Reign of the eastern emperor Justinian I, who attempts to regain some of the western Roman lands lost to the barbarians.

568

Another barbarian tribe, the Lombards, takes control of northern and central Italy.

1453
The Ottoman Turks besiege, sack, and seize control of Constantinople, marking the official end of the last remnant of the Roman Empire.

1776–1788
The distinguished English historian Edward Gibbon publishes his massive and brilliant *Decline and Fall of the Roman Empire*, initiating a flurry of fervid study and debate about Rome's fall that has continued unabated to the present.

For Further Research

Ancient Sources Relating
to Rome's Decline and Fall

Paul J. Alexander, ed., *The Ancient World: To 300 A.D.* New York: Macmillan, 1963.

Ammianus Marcellinus, *History*, published as *The Later Roman Empire, A.D. 354–378*. Trans. and ed., Walter Hamilton. New York: Penguin Books, 1986.

Augustan History, published as *Lives of the Later Caesars, The First Part of the* Augustan History, *With Newly Compiled* Lives *of Nerva and Trajan*. Trans. Anthony Birley. New York: Penguin Books, 1976.

Nels M. Bailkey, ed., *Readings in Ancient History: From Gilgamesh to Diocletian*. Lexington, MA: D.C. Heath, 1976.

Leon Bernard and Theodore B. Hodges, eds., *Readings in European History*. New York: Macmillan, 1958.

Dio Cassius, *Roman History*, excerpted in *The Roman History: The Reign of Augustus*. Trans. Ian Scott-Kilvert. New York: Penguin Books, 1987.

J. Wight Duff and Arnold M. Duff, trans., *Minor Latin Poets*. Cambridge, MA: Harvard University Press, 1968.

Eusebius, *Ecclesiastical History*. 2 vols. Trans. Roy J. Deferrari. Washington, D.C.: Catholic University of America Press, 1955.

Jerome, *Letters*, excerpted in F.A. Wright, trans., *Select Letters of St. Jerome*. Cambridge, MA: Harvard University Press, 1963.

Lactantius, *The Deaths of the Persecutors*, in Sister Mary Francis McDonald, trans., *Lactantius: Minor Works*. Washington, D.C.: Catholic University of America Press, 1965.

Naphtali Lewis and Meyer Reinhold, eds., *Roman Civilization, Sourcebook II: The Empire*. New York: Harper and Row, 1966.

Suetonius, *Lives of the Twelve Caesars*, published as *The Twelve Caesars*. Trans. Robert Graves, rev. Michael Grant. New York: Penguin Books, 1979.

Tacitus, *Germania*, in H. Mattingly, trans., *Tacitus On Britain and Germany*. Baltimore: Penguin Books, 1954.

Brian Tierney, ed., *The Middle Ages, Volume I: Sources of Medieval History*. New York: Knopf, 1973.

Modern Sources

Constantine and the Triumph of Christianity

Timothy D. Barnes, *Constantine and Eusebius*. Cambridge, MA: Harvard University Press, 1981.

Peter Brown, *Power and Persuasion in Late Antiquity: Towards A Christian Empire*. Madison: University of Wisconsin Press, 1992.

Owen Chadwick, *A History of Christianity*. New York: St. Martin's Press, 1995.

Garth Fowden, *Empire to Commonwealth: Consequences of Monotheism in Late Antiquity*. Princeton, NJ: Princeton University Press, 1993.

Michael Grant, *Constantine the Great: The Man and His Times*. New York: Scribner's, 1994.

A.H.M. Jones, *Constantine and the Conversion of Europe*. Toronto: University of Toronto Press, 1978.

Ramsay MacMullen, *Constantine*. New York: Dial Press, 1969.

Jaroslav Pelikan, *The Excellent Empire: The Fall of Rome and the Triumph of the Church*. San Francisco: Harper and Row, 1987.

Stewart Perowne, *Caesars and Saints: The Rise of the Christian State, A.D. 180–313*. New York: Barnes and Noble, 1962. Reprinted 1992.

General Studies of the Roman Empire

Lesley Adkins and Roy A. Adkins, *Handbook to Life in Ancient Rome*. New York: Facts On File, 1994.

Arthur E.R. Boak and William G. Sinnegin, *A History of Rome to 565 A.D.* New York: Macmillan, 1965.

Matthew Bunson, *A Dictionary of the Roman Empire*. Oxford, England: Oxford University Press, 1991.

Tim Cornell and John Matthews, *Atlas of the Roman World*. New York: Facts On File, 1982.

Donald R. Dudley, *The Civilization of Rome*. New York: New American Library, 1962.

Will Durant, *Caesar and Christ: A History of Roman Civilization and of Christianity from Their Beginnings to A.D. 325*. New York: Simon and Schuster, 1944.

Charles Freeman, *Egypt, Greece, and Rome: Civilizations of the Ancient Mediterranean*. Oxford, England: Oxford University Press, 1996.

——, *The World of the Romans*. New York: Oxford University Press, 1993.

Michael Grant, *The Climax of Rome*. New York: New American Library, 1968.

——, *Founders of the Western World: A History of Greece and Rome*. New York: Scribner's, 1991.

——, *History of Rome*. New York: Scribner's, 1978.

——, *The Roman Emperors*. New York: Barnes and Noble, 1997.

Anthony Kamm, *The Romans: An Introduction*. London: Routledge, 1995.

Naphtali Lewis, *Life in Egypt Under Roman Rule*. Oxford, England: Clarendon Press, 1983.

Harold Mattingly, *Roman Imperial Civilization*. New York: W.W. Norton, 1957.

Michael I. Rostovtzeff, *Social and Economic History of the Roman Empire* (2 volumes). Oxford, England: Oxford University Press, 1957.

Chris Scarre, *Chronicle of the Roman Emperors*. New York: Thames and Hudson, 1995.

Chester G. Starr, *Civilization and the Caesars*. New York: Norton, 1965.

——, *The Roman Empire, 27 B.C.–A.D. 476: A Study in Survival*. New York: Oxford University Press, 1982.

——, *A History of the Ancient World*. New York: Oxford University Press, 1991.

Colin Wells, *The Roman Empire*. Stanford, CA: Stanford University Press, 1984.

L.P. Wilkinson, *The Roman Experience*. Lanham, MD: University Press of America, 1974.

The Later Empire and Causes of Its Decline

Arthur E.R. Boak, *Manpower Shortage and the Fall of the Roman Empire in the West*. Westport, CT: Greenwood Press, 1955. Reprinted 1974.

Peter Brown, *The Making of Late Antiquity*. Cambridge, MA: Harvard University Press, 1978.

J.B. Bury, *History of the Later Roman Empire, 395–565*. 2 vols. New York: Dover, 1957.

Averil Cameron, *The Later Roman Empire: A.D. 284–430*. Cambridge, MA: Harvard University Press, 1993.

Mortimer Chambers, ed., *The Fall of the Roman Empire: Can It Be Explained?* New York: Holt, Rinehart, and Winston, 1963.

Edward Gibbon, *The Decline and Fall of the Roman Empire*. First published 1776–1788. 3 vols. Ed. David Womersley. New York: Penguin Books, 1994.

Michael Grant, *The Collapse and Recovery of the Roman Empire*. London: Routledge, 1999.

——, *The Fall of the Roman Empire*. New York: Macmillan, 1990.

——, *The Severans*. London: Routledge, 1996.

Donald Kagan, ed., *Decline and Fall of the Roman Empire: Why Did It Collapse?* Boston: D.C. Heath, 1962.

A.H.M. Jones, *The Decline of the Ancient World*. London: Longman Group, 1966. Note: This is a shortened (but still substantial) version of Jones's *The Later Roman Empire, 284–602*. 3 vols. Norman: University of Oklahoma Press, 1964. Reprinted 1975.

Ramsay MacMullen, *Corruption and the Decline of Rome*. New Haven, CT: Yale University Press, 1988.

——, *Roman Government's Response to Crisis: A.D. 235–337*. New Haven, CT: Yale University Press, 1976.

John Matthews, *The Roman Empire of Ammianus*. Baltimore: Johns Hopkins University Press, 1989.

Don Nardo, *The Decline and Fall of the Roman Empire*. San Diego: Lucent Books, 1998.

Stewart Perowne, *The End of the Roman World*. New York: Thomas Y. Crowell, 1966.

Paul Veyne, ed., *From Pagan Rome to Byzantium*, vol. 1 of Philippe Ariès and Georges Duby, eds., *A History of Private Life*. Cambridge, MA: Harvard University Press, 1987.

F.W. Walbank, *The Awful Revolution: The Decline of the Roman Empire in the West*. Toronto: University of Toronto Press, 1969.

Alaric Watson, *Aurelian and the Third Century*. London: Routledge, 1999.

Lynn White, Jr., ed., *The Transformation of the Roman World: Gibbon's Problem after Two Centuries*. Berkeley: University of California Press, 1966.

Romans Versus Barbarians

J.B. Bury, *Invasion of Europe by the Barbarians*. New York: Norton, 1967.

Arther Ferrill, *The Fall of the Roman Empire: The Military Explanation*. New York: Thames and Hudson, 1986.

Walter Goffart, *Barbarians and Romans, A.D. 418–584: The Techniques of Accommodation*. Princeton, NJ: Princeton University Press, 1980.

Michael Grant, *The Army of the Caesars*. New York: M. Evans and Company, 1974.

Peter Heather, *The Goths*. Cambridge, MA: Blackwell Publishing, 1996.

Edward N. Luttwak, *The Grand Strategy of the Roman Empire*. Baltimore: Johns Hopkins University Press, 1976.

Justine Davis Randers-Pehrson, *Barbarians and Romans: The Birth Struggle of Europe, A.D. 400–700*. Norman: University of Oklahoma Press, 1983.

Pat Southern and Karen R. Dixon, *The Late Roman Army*. New Haven, CT: Yale University Press, 1996.

E.A. Thompson, *Romans and Barbarians: The Decline of the Western Empire*. Madison: University of Wisconsin Press, 1982.

Survival of Roman Civilization in the East and West

Norman H. Baynes and H.St.L.B. Moss, *Byzantium: An Introduction to East Roman Civilization*. Oxford, England: Oxford University Press, 1961.

Peter Brown, *The World of Late Antiquity, A.D. 150–750*. New York: Harcourt Brace, 1971.

John Drinkwater and Hugh Elton, eds., *Fifth-Century Gaul: A Crisis in Identity?* Cambridge: Cambridge University Press, 1992.

Michael Grant, *From Rome to Byzantium: The Fifth Century A.D.* London: Routledge, 1998.

Alfred F. Havighurst, ed., *The Pirenne Thesis: Analysis, Criticism, and Revision.* Lexington, MA: D.C. Heath, 1969.

R.M. Haywood, *Myth of Rome's Fall.* Westport, CT: Greenwood, 1979.

Walter E. Kaegi, Jr., *Byzantium and the Decline of Rome.* Princeton, NJ: Princeton University Press, 1968.

Solomon Katz, *The Decline of Rome and the Rise of Medieval Europe.* Ithaca, NY: Cornell University Press, 1955.

Ferdinand Lot, *The End of the Ancient World and the Beginnings of the Middle Ages.* New York: Harper and Row, 1961.

John Julius Norwich, *Byzantium: The Early Centuries.* New York: Knopf, 1989.

——, *A Short History of Byzantium.* New York: Knopf, 1997.

Joseph Vogt, *The Decline of Rome: The Metamorphosis of Ancient Civilization.* Translated by Janet Sondheimer. London: Weidenfeld and Nicolson, 1967.

Index

About the Editor

Don Nardo has written numerous volumes about the ancient Roman world, including *The Punic Wars*, *The Collapse of the Roman Republic*, *Life of a Roman Slave*, *Rulers of Ancient Rome*, and biographies of Julius Caesar and Cleopatra. He resides with his wife Christine in Massachusetts.